REVISE AQA GCSE English Language

REVISION GUIDE

Series Consultant: Harry Smith

Authors: Jonathan Morgan, Julie Hughes and David Grant

Reviewer: David Grant

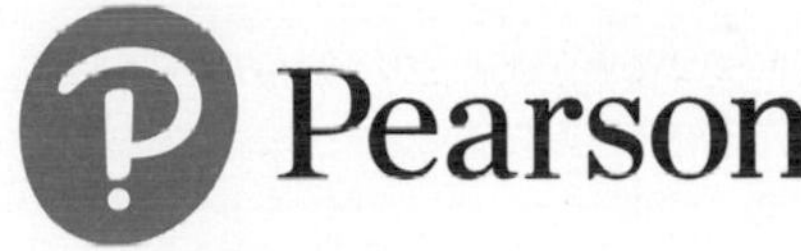

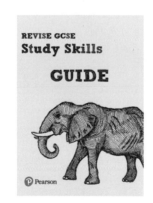

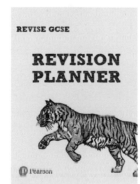

Contents

1-to-1 page match with the English Language Revision Workbook
ISBN 9781447987833

A small bit of small print
AQA publishes Sample Assessment Material and the Specification on its website. This is the official content and this book should be used in conjunction with it. The questions in *Now try this* have been written to help you practise every topic in the book. Remember: the real exam questions may not look like this.

The exam papers explained

The **English Language GCSE** consists of two exam papers: **Paper 1** and **Paper 2**. Make sure you know what to expect from each exam paper.

Paper 1: Explorations in creative reading and writing

Section A: Reading – 40 marks (25% of exam)

- You will read **one literature fiction text** from the **20th or 21st century**.
- You will answer **four questions**.

Section B: Writing – 40 marks (25% of exam)

- You will produce **one piece of descriptive or narrative piece of writing**.
- The **topic will be linked to the reading text** in Section A.
- You will **choose between two tasks**.
- One of the tasks will have a **visual stimulus** to help you think of ideas.

Paper 2: Writers' viewpoints and perspectives

Section A: Reading – 40 marks (25% of exam)

- You will read **one non-fiction text** and one literary non-fiction.
- One text will be from the **19th century**; the other from the **20th or 21st century**.
- You will answer **four questions**.

Section B: Writing – 40 marks (25% of exam)

- You will produce **one piece of writing**.
- The **theme will be linked to Section A**.
- You will write for a **specific audience and purpose**, and in a **specific form**.

Getting it right

Remember these top tips:

- Take highlighter pens in different colours to annotate the texts and questions.
- In the margins, write how much time you should spend on each question.
- Don't write too fast – this can make your handwriting harder to read.
- Keep your writing focused on the question – re-read the question and your answer. Ignore distractions – focus on your answers and showing off your skills.

Keeping it healthy

Before the exam:

- avoid caffeine and chocolate – these can lead to headaches
- get some fresh air – this will help to clear your head.

In the exam:

- stay hydrated – take water with you, but don't drink too much as a toilet trip will be distracting mid-exam
- breathe slowly and deeply to keep calm.

Developing your wider reading skills

All the texts in the exam will be 'unseen', so you won't have studied them in advance. Prepare by:

- reading a newspaper article every day
- reading a range of biographies and autobiographies
- finding a variety of texts from the 19th, 20th and 21st centuries on a similar theme for comparison.

Developing your writing knowledge

Develop your skills by:

- collecting examples of writing across a range of genres, including biography, diary, travel writing, novel openings, articles, information sheets
- experimenting with writing for different audiences – for example the elderly or teenagers
- practising writing with a different purpose in mind, for example to describe or argue.

Now try this

Your friend has asked you for some **last-minute** exam preparation advice. List the **five** things you think are the most important to remember just before or during the exam.

Had a look ☐ Nearly there ☐ Nailed it! ☐

Planning your exam time

Planning your time in the exam is extremely important. Running out of time is one of the most common ways that students lose marks in their exam. You should plan your time to get the most out of every minute.

Managing your time

Paper 1 and Paper 2 are both **1 hour and 45 minutes** long. This includes planning time and checking time. For each paper, make sure you **allow time to plan** your writing in Section B. Leave enough time to **check your answers** in both Section A and Section B. You could divide your time as shown below.

Paper 1

Question	Marks	Time
Reading and planning	–	15 mins
Section A: 1	4	5 mins
Section A: 2	8	10 mins
Section A: 3	8	10 mins
Section A: 4	20	20 mins
Section B: 5	40	Total: 45 mins Planning: 5 mins Writing: 35 mins Checking: 5 mins

Paper 2

Question	Marks	Time
Reading and planning	–	15 mins
Section A: 1	4	5 mins
Section A: 2	8	8 mins
Section A: 3	12	12 mins
Section A: 4	16	Total: 20 mins Planning: 5 mins Writing: 15 mins
Section B: 5	40	Total: 45 mins Planning: 5 mins Writing: 35 mins Checking: 5 mins

The first 15 minutes

Use the first 15 minutes of reading time well:

1. **Read the questions** to find out what you're looking for when you read the sources, highlighting key words.
2. **Skim read the sources** to get a rough idea of the main ideas.
3. **Read the sources closely,** including any **introductory information,** as this may give you **important clues about the genre, form, purpose and target audience**.
4. As you read closely, **highlight different features** that will help you answer the questions.
5. **Annotate the sources** with brief notes that relate to the questions.

If you find you are reading the sources without anything sinking in, stop, take a breath and start again, this time reading more slowly.

Now try this

1 Which questions should you spend about five minutes answering?
2 For which question should you spend about 15 minutes writing?
3 How can you get a rough idea of the main ideas in a source text?
4 What should you do if you are reading the sources but nothing is sinking in?
5 For each paper:
(a) How many marks are awarded in total for reading?
(b) How many marks are awarded in total for writing?

Paper 1 Reading questions 1

In **Paper 1, Section A: Reading**, you will need to answer **four questions**. The questions on this page are sample questions and do not need to be answered. Instead, focus on understanding what these question types are asking you to do. Then try the *Now try this* activity.

Question 1

This exam-style question is about **source 2**, *To Kill a Mockingbird*, which is a fiction text from the 20th century. Full text on page 102.

> **1** Read the first part of source 2, **lines 1 to 9**.
> List **four** things from this part of the text that give a negative picture of Maycomb. **(4 marks)**

This question directs you to a specific part of the source. Only look at these lines for your answer.

This means you only need to list your points. You don't need to explain or analyse them.

Assessment objective 1

Question 1 tests **assessment objective 1**:
- Identify and interpret explicit and implicit information and ideas.
- Select and synthesise evidence from different texts.

This assessment objective tests your ability to:
- find information in a text
- explain what is being communicated explicitly
- infer what is being suggested.

Question 2

> **2** How does the writer use language here to present Manderley as somewhere to be feared?
> You could include the writer's choice of:
> - words and phrases
> - language features and techniques
> - sentence forms. **(8 marks)**

You will need to stay focused on the question, use evidence to support your analysis and consider how the writer's choice of **vocabulary**, **sentence structure** and **language features** are used to create particular effects.

You can use the bullet points to help you structure your response, though you can use your own ideas too.

Assessment objective 2

Question 2 tests **assessment objective 2**:
- Explain, comment on and analyse how writers use language and structure to achieve effects and influence readers, using relevant subject terminology to support their views.

This assessment objective tests your ability to:
- pick out specific language features that are used by the writer to achieve particular effects
- comment on how the text is organised and structured to impact on the reader.

Assessment objective 2 assesses your awareness of language and structure. Question 2 is asking you to focus on language.

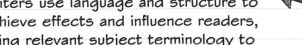

Now try this

Answer exam-style Question 1 above to test your skills in assessment objective 1.

Had a look ☐ Nearly there ☐ Nailed it! ☐

Paper 1 Reading questions 2

In **Paper 1, Section A: Reading**, you will need to answer **four questions**. The questions on this page are sample questions and do not need to be answered. Instead, focus on understanding what these question types are asking you to do.

Question 3

These exam-style questions are about **source 1**, *Rebecca*, which is a fiction text from the 20th century. Full text on page 101.

3 You now need to think about the **whole** of the **source**.
The text is from the opening of a novel.
How has the writer structured the text to interest you as a reader?
You could write about:

- how Manderley is introduced to the reader
- how the emotions of the narrator develop
- how the writer builds up interest in Manderley.

(8 marks)

For this question, you need to focus on the whole of the source.

You need to focus on how the text is **structured** and what effect this has, supporting your ideas with examples from the source.

The bullet points may help you structure your response, but you can also include your own ideas.

Like Paper 1, Question 2, this question tests **assessment objective 2**. Assessment objective 2 assesses your awareness of language and structure. This question is asking you to focus on structure.

For more about assessment objective 2, see page 3

Question 4

4 Focus this part of your answer on the second half of source 1, **from line 29 to the end**.
A student, having read this section of the text, commented: 'Manderley is presented as a threatening place rather than somewhere special.'
To what extent do you agree?
In your response, you could:

- write about your impressions of Manderley
- evaluate how the writer has created these impressions
- support your opinions with quotations from the text.

(20 marks)

You must only look at these specific lines for your answer.

You could consider alternative interpretations of the text; in this instance, you could find examples of Manderley being described as exciting and vibrant, as well as threatening and dangerous.

You could use the bullet points to help you structure your response.

Remember to provide direct quotations to support your evaluation.

Assessment objective 4

Question 4 tests **assessment objective 4**:

- Evaluate texts critically and support this with appropriate textual references.

This assessment objective tests your ability to:

- comment on the effectiveness of the writer's choices on the reader
- explain the ideas and viewpoint of the writer
- provide your own viewpoint
- use evidence to support your viewpoint.

Now try this

Look at exam-style Question 4 above. Find **three** quotations to support each of these viewpoints:

- Manderley is presented as a threatening place.
- Manderley is presented as a special place.

Paper 2 Reading questions 1

In **Paper 2, Section A: Reading**, you will need to answer **four questions**. The questions on this page are sample questions and do not need to be answered. Instead, focus on understanding what these question types are asking you to do. Then try the *Now try this* activity.

Question 1

This exam-style question is about **source 7a**, *On Women's Right to Vote*, which is a non-fiction text from the 19th century. Full text on page 109.

1 Read **source 7a**, from **lines 31 to 35**.
Choose **four** statements below which are TRUE.
- Shade the boxes of the ones that you think are true.
- Choose a maximum of four statements.
- The writer believes that:

A Women have too many rights. ☐
B Discrimination against women is wrong. ☐
C Women are not people. ☐
D Women should be treated equally. ☐
E Women are breaking the law. ☐
F There is only one question left to answer. ☐
G Women are citizens. ☐
H The state should enforce old laws. ☐

(4 marks)

This question directs you to a specific part of the source. Only look at these lines for your answer.

This means you only need to select the statements. You don't need to explain or analyse them.

Question 1 on Paper 2 tests assessment objective 1.

For more about assessment objective 1, see page 3

Question 2

This exam-style question is about **source 7a**, *On Women's Right to Vote* and **source 7b**, 'Suffragettes to Political Apathy'.

2 You need to refer to **source 7a** and **source 7b** for this question.
Use details from **both** sources. Write a summary of how the role of women is presented by both writers. **(8 marks)**

Make sure you select relevant evidence from both sources to support your ideas.

You need to summarise (synthesise) the ideas presented in the two sources.

For this question, you need to refer to both sources.

For more about synthesis, see pages 40–41

Question 2 on Paper 2 tests assessment objective 1.

Now try this

Answer exam-style Question 1 above to test your skills in assessment objective 1.

Had a look ☐ Nearly there ☐ Nailed it! ☐

Paper 2 Reading questions 2

In **Paper 2, Section A: Reading**, you will need to answer **four questions**. The questions on this page are sample questions and do not need to be answered. Instead, focus on understanding what these question types are asking you to do.

Question 3

This exam-style question is about **source 5a**, *The state of the Prisons, 1818*. Full text on page 105.

> **3** You need to refer **only** to **source 5a**.
> How does the writer use language to create sympathy for prisoners? **(12 marks)**

This question tests **assessment objective** 2. Assessment objective 2 assesses your awareness of language and structure. This question is asking you to focus on language.

No line numbers are given, so you need to refer to the whole source. However, make sure you select relevant information only – don't summarise the events.

It is not enough just to identify the techniques used. You need to **analyse the language** and comment on its effect on the reader. Make sure you refer to a **range** of language features to support your analysis.

For more about assessment objective 2, see page 3; for more about language features, see pages 19–23

Question 4

This exam-style questions is about **source 7a**, *On Women's Right to Vote*. Full text on page 109.

> **4** For this question, you need to refer to the **whole of source 7a** together with **source 7b**.
> Compare how the two writers convey their different attitudes towards the role of women.
> In your answer, you should:
> - compare their different attitudes
> - compare the methods they use to convey their attitudes
> - support your ideas with quotations from both texts. **(16 marks)**

You need to consider both sources equally, but make sure you only focus on parts of the texts that are relevant to the question.

Make sure you use the bullet points as a guide. You can add your own observations too, but keep focused on the question.

This means what the writers believe in and what their viewpoints are.

This means 'to get across' or 'to communicate'.

This refers to the range of language and structural techniques the writers use to get their ideas across.

You need to find similarities and differences between the sources, using quotations from both sources to support your analysis.

Assessment objective 3

Question 4 tests **assessment objective 3**:

- Compare writers' ideas and perspectives, as well as how they are conveyed, across two or more texts.

This assessment objective tests your ability to:

- identify, comment on and compare writers' ideas and perspectives
- analyse and compare **how** writers convey their ideas and perspectives.

Now try this

Look at exam-style Question 4 above, then answer these questions:

1 How many of the two sources should you write about?
2 How much of each source should you use for your answer?
3 What are the key words in the question that tell you what to do?
4 What views or attitudes in the sources is this question asking you to write about?
5 How long should you spend on this question?

Skimming for the main idea

Maximise the time available in the exam by **skim reading**. First, skim the texts for their main idea and to understand the purpose, content and target audience. Then follow up with a second, more detailed reading. In particular, skim reading will help you with the **non-fiction** sources in **Paper 2**.

Key features

Look at these key places when you skim read a text.

The heading

The first sentence of each paragraph

The last sentence of the text

21st

From Suffragettes to Political apathy: why it is essential that women exercise their votes

In 1928, after years of peaceful campaigning and militant tactics alike, a group of now-famous, inspirational women called The Suffragettes achieved their goals: women in the UK over the age of 21 were granted the right to vote. For women everywhere this was a remarkable step…

In the 2010 Election, only 64% of women exercised their right to vote, compared to 66% of men, highlighting that although lower voter turnout is a problem facing the UK as a whole, it affects females more greatly. With the May 2015 General Election fast approaching…

For both genders, it is important to remember that in our current international political system, voting is increasingly making a difference. Things such as the recent Greek election…

Register to vote in the May 2015 General Election now.

Getting it right

To make your skim reading even more useful, read the questions carefully first. The questions will give you clues about the main ideas or themes in the texts.

Summing up

Think about how you could sum up the text in one or two sentences. Here are some ideas for the text on the right:

There are pros and cons to restorative justice programmes.

Restorative justice can reduce offending but is only effective for minor crimes.

Remember to look at:

- the heading
- the first sentence of each paragraph
- the last sentence of the text.

21st

Extract from 'Prison doesn't work'. Full text on page 106. Lines 44–52.

Campaigners for restorative justice programmes where offenders engage with the impact of their crime and often meet their victims – say it can reduce reoffending by up to 27%. A government analysis puts the improvement at a more conservative 14%. One important limitation on restorative justice is that it is only considered effective for more minor crimes such as burglary. Restorative justice isn't used for offences like domestic violence, murder or rape.

Now try this

Skim read **source 5a**, *The state of the Prisons, 1818*, on page 105. Try not to spend more than 30 seconds skim reading. Can you sum up the main idea in **one** sentence, or at most **two**?

Had a look ☐ Nearly there ☐ Nailed it! ☐

Annotating the sources

For **both papers**, get into the habit of **highlighting, underlining or circling** parts of a source that you can use to support your answers.

Highlight and annotate

Look at this **Paper 1** exam-style question about the extract from *To Kill a Mockingbird.*

> **2** Look in detail at this extract from **lines 1 to 5** of the source.
> How does the writer use language here to create an impression of Maycomb?
> You could include the writer's choice of:
> - words and phrases
> - language features and techniques
> - sentence forms. **(8 marks)**

Don't just highlight useful quotes. For each highlight, note down:

- the effect on the reader
- the technique used to achieve it.

Try to use the correct technical language if you know it.

20th

Extract from To Kill a Mockingbird. *Full text on page 102. Lines 1–5.*

Maycomb was an old town, but it was a tired old town when I first knew it. In rainy weather the streets turned to red slop; grass grew on the sidewalks, the courthouse sagged in the square. Somehow, it was hotter then: a black dog suffered on a summer's day; bony mules hitched to Hoover carts flicked flies in the sweltering shade of the live oaks on the square. Men's stiff collars wilted by nine in the morning. Ladies bathed before noon, after their three-o'clock naps, and by nightfall were like soft teacakes with frostings of sweat and sweet talcum.

You can gather information for your answer by annotating the source like this:

- Repeated phrase 'old town' suggests a monotonous, run-down place.
- Suggests neglect, lack of care.
- Verbs – sagged/suffered/wilted – create a negative tone; foreshadowing future events?
- Adjective 'sweltering' adds to the sense of oppressive summer heat.
- Use of the simile reflects the meaningless existence.

Now try this

Read the extract on the right from *Rebecca* (lines 44–48). It describes the house, Manderley. Quickly highlight and annotate any words or phrases from this extract that you could use to answer this **Paper 1** exam-style question:

> **2** Look in detail at this extract from **lines 44 to 48** of the source.
> How does the writer use language here to create an impression of Manderley?
> You could include the writer's choice of:
> - words and phrases
> - language features and techniques
> - sentence forms. **(8 marks)**

20th

Nettles were everywhere, the vanguard of the army. They choked the terrace, they sprawled about the paths, they leant, vulgar and lanky, against the very windows of the house. They made indifferent sentinels, for in many places their ranks had been broken by the rhubarb plant, and they lay with crumpled heads and listless stems, making a pathway for the rabbits. I left the drive and went on to the terrace, for the nettles were no barrier to me, a dreamer. I walked enchanted, and nothing held me back.

Putting it into practice

In **Paper 1, Section A: Reading**, you'll need to respond to the impact of the writer's **language choices** in a **fiction** text. Read **source 3**, *Every Man For Himself*, on page 103. Then read the exam-style question below and look at how a student has used annotation to help them respond to it.

Commenting on language

For a question like this you should:

- ✓ spend about 10 minutes on your answer
- ✓ highlight key words in the question so that you get the focus right
- ✓ use only the lines of text referred to in the question
- ✓ focus on the way the writer has used words and sentences to create ideas about the narrator in the mind of the reader.

Worked example

2 Look in detail at this extract from **lines 3 to 15** of the source.
How does the writer use language here to give the reader an impression of the narrator?
You could include the writer's choice of:

- words and phrases
- language features and techniques
- sentence forms. **(8 marks)**

In the exam, you should try to comment on sentence forms as well as vocabulary choices.

For more about sentences, see pages 31–32

The narrator is presented as very determined, as he is 'clinging' to the ladder even though he is unsteady, 'like a flag on a pole'. This gives the impression that he is trying hard in difficult circumstances. He is prepared to 'make a leap for it', which suggests that he is brave, and he is a good friend, checking on his friends – Hopper and Scurra – and putting them first. The words 'some inner voice' suggest he has good instincts under pressure.

The more focused annotations in this answer extract lead to a focused and detailed response to the question. Take the time to annotate the text to help you write a stronger answer.

These are the sections of the text that a student highlighted, with the student's annotations.

Clinging... I tried to climb to the roof... waved like a flag on a pole

Determined, tries even though unsteady

I thought I must make a leap for it...

'Leap' suggests he is brave

... turned to look for Hopper... saw Scurra again, one arm hooked through the rail to steady himself.

Checks on friends, puts others first

... some inner voice...

Has good instincts under pressure

Now try this

Complete the 'Sample answer extract' on *Every Man for Himself* above. Aim to identify at least **two** more relevant points.

Putting it into practice

In **Paper 2, Section A: Reading**, you'll need to respond to the impact of a writer's **language choices** in a **non-fiction** text. Read **source 5a**, *The state of the Prisons, 1818*, on page 105. Then read the exam-style question below and look at how a student has used annotation to help them respond to it.

Worked example

3 You now need to refer **only** to **source 5a**.
How does the writer use language to create sympathy for the prisoners? **(12 marks)**

In the exam, you should try to comment on sentence forms as well as vocabulary choices.

The writer uses the adjective 'wretched' to create the impression that the treatment of the prisoners is inhumane, which helps to evoke the sympathy of the reader. The alliteration and emotive adjectives in 'impudent and insulting' and 'disgusting and depraved' are used to present the prisoner as being ridiculed and tormented, heightening the reader's sympathy further. In addition, the negative verbs 'exposed' and 'hammered' are used to reflect the mistreatment of the prisoner.

Note how the focused highlights and annotations in this answer extract lead to a focused and detailed response to the question. Language features are referred to and their impact on the reader is considered. Take the time to annotate the text to help you write a stronger answer.

Commenting on language

For a question like this you should:

- spend about 12 minutes on your answer
- highlight key words in the question so that you get the focus right
- check if you should comment on the whole text or only certain lines referred to in the question
- focus on how language is used effectively to influence the reader.

These are the sections of the text that a student highlighted, with the student's annotations.

... wretched...

Adjective creates the impression the treatment is inhumane – helping to create sympathy.

... impudent and insulting boys... disgusting and depraved...

Alliteration and emotive adjectives used to present the prisoner as ridiculed and tormented – heightens sympathy.

... exposed... hammered ...

Negative verbs reflect the sense of the prisoner being mistreated.

Now try this

Continue the 'Sample answer extract' on *The state of the Prisons, 1818* above. Aim to identify at least **three** more relevant points.

The writer's viewpoint

For **Paper 2**, you will need to think about the writer's viewpoint. If you can identify a writer's viewpoint, you will be able to understand their ideas and comment on how the writer has expressed them.

Identifying the writer's viewpoint

Decide whether the viewpoint is positive or negative.

The heading, opening sentence and any subheadings in a text are all useful places to get an idea of the writer's viewpoint.

Viewpoint

A **viewpoint** is the writer's attitude and opinion on a particular subject.

- Most texts reveal something about the writer's viewpoint.
- But in some texts the writer gives the facts as clearly as possible without revealing their own viewpoint. These texts are **unbiased**.

Look closely at the following to develop your understanding:

- **The heading:** clearly expresses the writer's view that more women should vote.
- **The writer's choice of language:** immediate focus on the suffragettes as 'inspirational'.
- **The writer's choice of ideas:** opening paragraph focuses on the contrast between the historical struggle for the vote and the need for women today to do more to change society.

21st

Extract from 'From Suffragettes to Political Apathy', lines 3–11. Full text on page 110.

From Suffragettes to Political Apathy: why it is essential that women exercise their votes

In 1928, after years of peaceful campaigning and militant tactics alike, a group of now-famous, inspirational women called The Suffragettes achieved their goals: women in the UK over the age of 21 were granted the right to vote. For women everywhere this was a remarkable step: they had the opportunity to change society. ... Today, we still live in a society where men dominate much of the public and political spheres, but women also have the power to change some of the policies that constrain us.

Now try this

Read this extract from the next paragraph of the article from **source 7b** 'From Suffragettes to Political Apathy' lines 12–17. How does it tell you more about the writer's point of view?

Write **one** or **two** sentences commenting on the writer's:

- choice of ideas
- use of language.

21st

In the 2010 Election, only 64% of women exercised their right to vote, compared to 66% of men, highlighting that although lower voter turnout is a problem facing the UK as a whole, it affects females more greatly. With the May 2015 General Election fast approaching, in a time when politicians and citizens alike are concerned about voter apathy, and celebrity Russell Brand – who encourages people not to vote because politics is 'corrupt' – gaining support, it is time to reflect on the values that these important women stood for.

Had a look ☐ Nearly there ☐ Nailed it! ☐

Fact, opinion and expert evidence

For **Paper 2**, you will need to think about how writers make their ideas more **persuasive** or **convincing** by supporting them with **facts, opinions and expert evidence**. Think carefully about the facts and opinions in a text, as writers can sometimes use them in a misleading way in order to present a particular point of view.

fact *noun*
1. Something that can be **proved** to be true.
'Manchester is a city in the United Kingdom.'

opinion
An idea or viewpoint that the writer or speaker **believes** to be true.
'Manchester is the greatest city on earth.'

expert evidence
Facts or opinions provided by an expert on the subject.
'Barry Chesham, a travel writer with over 30 years' experience, says: "Manchester is the greatest city on earth."'

Getting it right

Referring to how the writer has used facts, opinions and expert evidence can improve your answers.

Finding facts, opinions and expert evidence

Read the extract from **source 5b** 'Prison doesn't work' below. In this article, the writer:

- makes his viewpoint clear by giving his **opinion** in the subheading
- refers to **expert evidence** to back up his opinion
- supports his opinion with **facts.**

Look out for facts that take the form of statistics.

21st

Extract from 'Prison doesn't work', lines 53–69. Full text on page 106.

Why does prison work so badly?

Prison reformers such as the Prison Reform Trust point to demographics of our prisoners as part of the problem: poor education, mental health problems and fewer options for getting their life back on the straight and narrow.

But there are also some simple things that the prison and probation services can do that make things better. Those involve helping prisoners maintain connections with the outside world.

Prison reformers point to the differences between offenders leaving prison after a long time and those leaving prison after a short sentence. Offenders who leave after a longer time get more help readjusting to normal life. Those on shorter sentences don't.

And as we mention above, reoffending rates are significantly higher
for people given short term sentences than those given ones over a year.

Now try this

Make sure you know the difference between a fact, an opinion and expert evidence.

Read the whole of **source 5b**, 'Prison doesn't work', on page 106. Note down **one** further fact, **one** further opinion and **one** further piece of expert evidence that the writer uses to support his viewpoint.

Explicit information and ideas

In **both papers**, you will be tested on whether you can identify and interpret **explicit** and **implicit** information and ideas.

explicit *adjective*
1. Stated clearly and in detail, leaving no room for confusion or doubt.
'the arrangement had not been made explicit'
Synonyms: clear, direct, plain, obvious, straightforward, clear-cut, crystal clear, clearly expressed, easily understandable, blunt

'Explicit' means you **don't** need to look for **hidden meanings or provide any explanations.** If you are asked to list examples from the source – as in **Paper 1, Question 1** – you just need to find **short quotations** or **paraphrase** (put into your own words) what is clearly there. Keep your answers as brief as possible – avoid writing in full sentences, exploring language or the impact on the reader.

This **Paper 1** exam-style question is about **source 4**, *The Help*, which is a fiction text from the 21st century.

Worked example

1 Read the extract from **source 4**.
List **four** duties that the narrator describes doing in this part of the text. **(4 marks)**

cooking
cleaning
getting babies to sleep
getting babies to stop crying

Explicit information from the text is either listed as short quotations or is paraphrased. Full sentences and explanations have been avoided.

21st

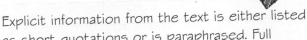

Extract from The Help. *Full text on page 104. Lines 1–4.*

Mae Mobley was born on a early Sunday morning in August, 1960. A church baby we like to call It. Taking care a white babies, that's what I do, along with all the cooking and the cleaning. I done raised seventeen kids in my lifetime. I know how to get them babies to sleep, stop crying, and go in the toilet bowl before they mamas even get out a bed in the morning.

In the exam, use your highlighter to find the correct answers quickly.

Now try this

Read the extract from **source 2** *To Kill a Mockingbird*, then answer this **Paper 1** exam-style question:

1 Read again the first part of the source, **lines 1 to 5**.
List **four** things from this part of the text about the effect of the heat in Maycomb. **(4 marks)**

20th

Extract from To Kill a Mockingbird. *Full text on page 102. Lines 1–5.*

Maycomb was an old town, but it was a tired old town when I first knew it. In rainy weather the streets turned to red slop; grass grew on the sidewalks, the courthouse sagged in the square. Somehow, it was hotter then: a black dog suffered on a summer's day; bony mules hitched to Hoover carts flicked flies in the sweltering shade of the live oaks on the square. Men's stiff collars wilted by nine in the morning. Ladies bathed before noon, after their three-o'clock naps, and by nightfall were like soft teacakes with frostings of sweat and sweet talcum.

Had a look ☐ Nearly there ☐ Nailed it! ☐

Implicit information and ideas

In **both papers**, you will be tested on whether you can identify and interpret **explicit** and **implicit** information and ideas.

implicit *adjective*
1. Suggested though not directly expressed 'comments seen as implicit criticism of the children'
Synonyms: implied, indirect, inferred, understood, hinted, suggested, deducible

Writers do not always state their meaning explicitly. Sometimes you will have to work out what the writer is **suggesting** or **implying** – in other words, what is **implicit** in the text. This is sometimes called making an **inference** and is also referred to as **reading between the lines**. In some cases, writers intend that their writing has more than one meaning.

This **Paper 2** exam-style question is about **source 7b**, 'From Suffragettes to Political Apathy', which is a non-fiction text from the 21st century.

Worked example

1 Read the extract from **source 7b**.
Choose **four** statements below which are TRUE.
- Shade the boxes of the ones that you think are true.
- Choose a maximum of four statements.

A In 1928, all women were allowed to vote. ☐
B Women over the age of 21 were allowed to vote in 1928. ☐
C Emmeline Pankhurst only campaigned peacefully. ☐
D The suffragettes used military tactics. ☐
E The writer admires the achievements of the suffragettes. ☐
F Men were unhappy that women were granted the right to vote in 1928. ☐
G The writer feels that the society we live in is still biased towards men. ☐
H Emmeline Pankhurst was elected in 1928. ☐

(4 marks)

B Women over the age of 21 were allowed to vote in 1928. — Explicit

D The suffragettes used military tactics. — Explicit

E The writer admires the achievements of the suffragettes. — Implicit

G The writer feels that the society we live in is still biased towards men. — Implicit

21st

Extract from 'From Suffragettes to Political Apathy'. Full text on page 110. Lines 3–11.

In 1928, after years of peaceful campaigning and militant tactics alike, a group of now-famous, inspirational women called The Suffragettes achieved their goals: women in the UK over the age of 21 were granted the right to vote. For women everywhere this was a remarkable step: they had the opportunity to change society. Emmeline Pankhurst once stated that the only way to create equality is "through giving women political power", which shows the way that these revolutionary feminists expected patriarchal society to change. They saw giving women the power to vote for the political leaders who decided the policies which dramatically affected their lives as fundamental. Today, we still live in a society where men dominate much of the public and political spheres, but women also have the power to change some of the policies that constrain us.

Now try this

Read lines 34–38 of **source 7b**, 'From Suffragettes to Political Apathy', on page 110. Then identify:
- **two** pieces of explicit information
- **two** implicit ideas.

Inference

In **both papers**, you will need to make **inferences** (read between the lines) when a question asks you to respond to the writer's choices and their impact on the reader. Remember, inference is about working out what the writer is **implying** (suggesting).

What is the writer implying?

Manderley is an important place as it features in regular dreams.

Suggests it is strongly protected and difficult to enter.

Suggests it has been empty for a while.

20th

Extract from Rebecca. *Full text on page 101. Lines 1–4.*

Last night I dreamt I went to Manderley again. It seemed to me I stood by the iron gate leading to the drive, and for a while I could not enter, for the way was barred to me. There was a padlock and a chain upon the gate. I called in my dream to the lodge-keeper, and had no answer, and peering closer through the rusted spokes of the gate I saw that the lodge was uninhabited.

This **Paper 1** exam-style question is about the extract from **source 1**, *Rebecca*.

Worked example

2 How does the writer use language here to describe Manderley?
You could include the writer's choice of:

- words and phrases
- language features and techniques
- sentence forms. **(8 marks)**

The first line suggests Manderley is an important place as the narrator has 'dreamt' of it 'again'. 'The iron gate' that is 'barred' to the narrator and padlocked suggests that Manderley is strongly protected and difficult to enter. The narrator sees that it is uninhabited and the fact that the spokes are 'rusted' suggests it may have been empty for some time and may be neglected. The overall impression given is that Manderley is a forbidding and frightening place and the narrator's dreams could well be nightmares.

Look out for bullet points in a question like this. You can use them to help you structure your response.

A fully developed answer should:

- refer to evidence from the source
- comment on what can be inferred from this evidence
- develop and summarise the point with further comments or additional evidence from the source.

Use **one-word quotations** where possible. This makes your inference really clear and specific.

For more about using evidence to evaluate texts, see page 37

Now try this

Read the next paragraph (lines 5–16) of **source 1**, *Rebecca*, on page 101. Write **one paragraph** to continue the worked example above. Use **two** or **three** carefully chosen and short quotations to support your answer.

Remember to keep exam-style question 2 above in mind. Choose quotations that clearly support the inferences you make.

Had a look ☐ Nearly there ☐ Nailed it! ☐

Point–Evidence–Explain

P-E-E is a technique you can use in your answers for **both papers** to make them clearer and better organised.

1. Make your **point**.
2. Provide **evidence** to support the point.
3. **Explain** how the evidence supports the point.

Getting it right

P-E-E is particularly useful when answering questions that ask you to:
- **comment** on language and structure
- **evaluate** a text
- **compare** texts.

P-E-E in practice

You should use a range of phrases to link your point, evidence and **explanation**.

1. Make your point: The writer uses | The article focuses on
2. Introduce your evidence: For example, | The writer describes | For instance,
3. Introduce your explanation: This gives the impression that | The writer is implying that | This suggests | This shows

This **Paper 2** exam-style question is about **source 7a**, *On Women's Right to Vote*.

19th

Extract from On Women's Right to Vote. *Full text on page 109. Lines 1–5.*

Friends and fellow citizens: I stand before you tonight under indictment for the alleged crime of having voted at the last presidential election, without having a lawful right to vote. It shall be my work this evening to prove to you that in thus voting, I not only committed no crime, but, instead, simply exercised my citizen's rights, guaranteed to me and all United States citizens by the National Constitution, beyond the power of any state to deny.

Worked example

3 How does the writer use language to persuade her audience that women should have the right to vote? **(12 marks)**

The writer addresses her audience in a way that encourages them to take her side. For example, she opens with 'Friends and fellow citizens' and refers to her 'alleged' crime. By using the word 'fellow', she is encouraging the audience to agree with her point of view. Similarly, her use of the adjective 'alleged' to describe the charge against her persuades the audience that there has been an injustice and encourages them to sympathise with her.

✓ The paragraph opens with a developed point that directly addresses the question.

✓ The adverbial 'For example' introduces two short, relevant quotations as evidence to support the point.

✓ The evidence is then explained in detail with a comment on the effect of the language on the reader.

Now try this

Read lines 14–16 from **source 7a**, *On Women's Right to Vote* on page 109. Then use the P-E-E structure to write **one paragraph** in answer to this **Paper 2** exam-style question:

3 You now need to refer **only** to **source 7a**. How does the writer use language to present her point of view? **(12 marks)**

Putting it into practice

In **Paper 1, Section A: Reading**, you'll need to respond to how writers use **language** to achieve particular **effects** in **fiction** texts. Read **source 3**, *Every Man For Himself*, on page 103. Then look at the exam-style question below and read the extracts from two students' answers.

Worked example

2 Look in detail at source 3, from **lines 8 to 16**.
How does the writer use language here to describe the danger the narrator is in?
You could include the writer's choice of:

- words and phrases
- language features and techniques
- sentence forms. **(8 marks)**

In the exam, you should try to comment on sentence forms as well as vocabulary choices.

For more about sentences, see pages 31–32

Commenting on language and structure

For a question like this you should:

- ✓ spend about 10 minutes on your answer
- ✓ read the question carefully and **highlight the main focus**
- ✓ only use the lines of text **referred to in the question**
- ✓ comment on **how** the writer uses language and structure and what the **effects** are on the reader.

Sample answer extract

The writer is really scared in this extract as he is described as being like a cork, which is really small. He grabs the grille really tight, which shows he is scared. He also hears sounds of the 'angry' sea, which makes him scared.

✗ Point is not made clearly – it is the narrator, not the writer, who is scared.

✓ Relevant reference to the text, though not always accurate ('angry' describes the roar of the ship, not the sea) and not developed.

Using P-E-E can help you structure your answer and ensure it includes a clear explanation of how your evidence supports your point.

Improved sample answer

The danger the narrator is in is made clear by the writer's use of language. Verbs such as 'staggered', 'tipped' and 'tossed' create an unsettling atmosphere and suggest a situation that is beyond control. The narrator also states 'I released my grip and let myself be carried away', which makes him seem powerless against the strength of the water.

✓ Point shows a clear focus on the question.

✓ Reference to specific language techniques and vocabulary choices, with relevant evidence used to support analysis.

✓ Clear explanation of the effect of the writer's language choices on the reader.

Note how this answer refers directly to the effect of the writer's choices on the reader.

Now try this

Complete the 'Improved sample answer' above. Aim to identify and explain **three** more relevant points.

Remember to:

- focus on the question
- refer to specific language techniques and vocabulary choices
- use relevant evidence to support your points
- explain the effects of the language the writer has used.

Had a look ☐ Nearly there ☐ Nailed it! ☐

Putting it into practice

In **Paper 2, Section A: Reading**, you'll need to respond to how writers use **language for effect** in **non-fiction** texts. Read **source 6a**, *Wonderful Adventures of Mrs. Seacole*, on page 107. Then look at the exam-style question below and read the extracts from two students' answers.

Worked example

3 How does the writer use language to encourage the reader to admire her? **(12 marks)**

In the exam, you should try to comment on sentence forms as well as vocabulary choices.

For more about sentences, see pages 31–32

Commenting on language

For a question like this you should:

- ✓ spend about 12 minutes on your answer
- ✓ highlight key words in the question so that you get the focus right
- ✓ refer to the whole of the source
- ✓ comment on **how** the writer uses language and what the **effects** are on the reader.

Sample answer extract

The writer wants the reader to think she's brave because she says 'we set to work bravely', which shows how brave and strong they were. She also says she was 'shaken in health' by what happened to her, which makes us think she is also brave for what she went through in the war.

✓ Evidence selected is relevant and clearly focused on the question.

✗ Explanation repeats the point and doesn't reveal an understanding of the effects of the writer's language choices on the reader.

Remember that P-E-E stands for **Point-Evidence-Explain**. You need to explain how your evidence supports the point you have made to make your answer complete and effective.

Improved sample answer

The writer uses the adverb 'bravely' and the alliteration in 'fallen fortunes' to reflect the enormity of the struggle she went through as a nurse in the Crimean War. This encourages the reader to admire her strength and courage. When the writer refers to the 'glow of pride' she felt, we are encouraged to respect her achievements as well as feel some sympathy for her not being rewarded for her achievements as she returns 'poor and helpless'.

✓ Specific reference to language techniques and vocabulary choices.

✓ A range of supporting evidence backs up the points made.

✓ Sophisticated language used to support the analysis.

✓ Clear and fully developed explanation that links back to the question.

Note how this strong answer varies the P-E-E structure while still including points, evidence and explanations.

Now try this

Continue the 'Improved sample answer' above. Aim to identify and explain **three** more relevant points.

Remember to:

- focus on the question
- refer to specific language techniques and vocabulary choices
- use relevant evidence to support your points
- explain the effects of the language the writer has used.

Word classes

In **both papers**, you will be asked to comment on the writers' **choices of language**. Start by thinking about the types of words – or **word classes** – writers use.

Nouns

These are words used to describe:

- objects: e.g. ladder, roof, ship, cork
- people: e.g. man, musician, Jem, mother
- places: e.g. Manderley, town, county
- ideas: e.g. justice, strength, determination.

Remember: **pronouns** replace or stand in for nouns – e.g. I, you, he, our, theirs.

Nouns indicating an idea are called abstract nouns.

Verbs

These are words used to describe:

- actions: e.g. to move, to play, to read
- occurrences: e.g. to live, to die
- states: e.g. to be, to know, to dream.

Adjectives

These are words to describe a noun: e.g. frosty, deafening, old, hot, dark.

Remember: **adjectives** can become **comparatives** giving degrees of difference (e.g. hotter, darker) and **superlatives** giving the most or least (e.g. hottest, darkest).

Adverbs

- **adverbs** describe verbs – e.g. slowly, clearly, desperately, gradually, often, sometimes. They are usually **(but not always)** formed by adding –ly to an adjective.
- **adverbs** can also modify adjectives and other adverbs.

Examples

Here are some student comments about the extracts opposite, focusing on word class:

Clinging to the rung of the ladder I tried to climb to the roof but there was such a sideways slant that I waved like a flag on a pole.

The writer uses verbs that are carefully chosen to focus the reader's mind on the danger the narrator faces.

To them this government is not a democracy. It is not a republic. It is an odious aristocracy…

The writer uses a list of three abstract nouns (democracy, republic, aristocracy) to reinforce her sense of injustice about women not having the right to vote. The juxtaposition of the words 'democracy' and 'aristocracy' help to present the gap between the rights of men and women.

Jem and I found our Father satisfactory: he played with us, read to us, and treated us with courteous detachment.

The writer uses the adjective 'courteous' and the abstract nouns 'satisfactory' and 'detachment' to present the functional relationship the children had with their father – secure though not affectionate.

Now try this

Read lines 12–14 of **source 2**, *To Kill a Mockingbird*, on page 102. Calpurnia is cook to the narrator's family and looks after the narrator, Scout.

Write **two** sentences about the relationship between Scout and Calpurnia, focusing on the writer's use of word class and its effect.

Connotations

Some words can create bigger ideas in our minds through the ideas and attitudes they suggest. These ideas and attitudes are called **connotations**.

Thinking about what a word or phrase suggests can help you to write effective comments on the writer's choice of language in **both papers**.

Look at what the phrase 'angry roaring' could suggest in the example opposite.

... the angry roaring of the dying ship...

The connotation of the phrase 'angry roaring' suggests the ship is like a furious beast. This, in turn, suggests the ship is large and distressed.

Language choice

These sentences have similar literal meanings. But the connotations let you know the writer's **real attitude**.

 The cold water pulled me down.

 The icy liquid dragged me down.

 The Arctic flow sucked me under.

Exploring the **connotations** of the language in a text can help you to write about the **impact** of the writer's **language choices** on the reader. In this example, the connotations of the writer's language choices tell you a great deal about the writer's **attitude** and the **atmosphere** he is trying to create.

Connotations in context

context *noun*
1. The parts of something written or spoken that immediately precede and follow a word or passage and clarify its meaning.

Getting it right

Words can have different meanings depending on their **context**: what comes before and after them in a text. Sometimes you need to think about the context to interpret the meaning of a word and understand its connotations. The context can also help you to make sense of unfamiliar words. (Note that we also use the term 'context' to talk about the time and place a text was written in.)

Extract from Every Man For Himself. *Full text on page 103. Lines 1–3.*

The stern began to lift from the water. Guggenheim and his valet played mountaineers, going hand over hand up the rail. The hymn turned ragged; ceased altogether. The musicians scrambled upwards, the spike of the cello scraping the deck.

This literally means people who climb mountains but here it carries connotations of bravery and daring, because they are climbing in such dangerous conditions.

This literally means torn and tattered but it also has connotations suggesting broken, uneven and ruined.

This has connotations of being unable to find a footing, and of needing to move quickly and desperately.

Now try this

Read lines 21–31 of **source 3**, *Every Man For Himself*, on page 103.
Write a brief sentence to explain the literal meaning and the connotation of each of these words:

silent howl | chilled | ghostly

Figurative language

In **Paper 1**, you will need to comment on the way writers use **language** to create **atmosphere** or to make readers feel a particular **emotion**. **Figurative language**, or **imagery**, is often used to create pictures in the reader's mind.

Comment on figurative language

Explaining the **effects** of the figurative language used in a text can help to improve your exam responses.

Getting it right

When you are commenting on figurative language, make sure you:

- give the **name** for the figurative device used if you know it
- comment on the **effect** of the language used.

simile *noun*
1. A figure of speech involving the comparison of one thing with another, usually using 'as' or 'like', used to make a description more vivid.

20th

Extract from Every Man For Himself. *Full text on page 103. Lines 8–9.*

As the ship staggered and tipped, a great volume of water flowed in over the submerged bows and tossed me like a cork to the roof.

The writer uses a simile to compare the narrator to something very light: a cork. This emphasises the power of the water and makes the narrator seem more vulnerable and defenceless. Corks are also a small, disposable item so it suggests that the narrator is powerless against the force of the water.

metaphor *noun*
1. A direct comparison suggesting a resemblance between one thing and another, used to build a vivid picture.

20th

Extract from Rebecca. *Full text on page 101. Line 17.*

The drive was a ribbon now, a thread of its former self, with gravel surface gone …

The writer uses a metaphor comparing the drive to a ribbon and a thread. This suggests the drive is no longer solid or capable of carrying vehicles and 'thread' suggests it has become narrow and fragile.

personification *noun*
1. Describing something non-human as if it were human.

20th

Extract from Rebecca. *Full text on page 101. Lines 44–45.*

Nettles were everywhere, the vanguard of the army. They choked the terrace, they sprawled about the paths, they leant, vulgar and lanky, against the very windows of the house.

The writer personifies the nettles by describing them as having human power to destroy everything in their path. This helps the writer to create a threatening tone.

Now try this

Read lines 36–38 of **source 1**, *Rebecca*, on page 101.
Write **two** or **three** sentences, commenting on:

- the atmosphere the writer creates
- how figurative language is used to create this atmosphere.

Remember to name the figurative device used if you can.

Had a look ☐ Nearly there ☐ Nailed it! ☐

Creation of character

For **Paper 1** you may be asked to comment on the way a writer has used **language** to create a particular **impression** of a **character**.

Character through action

What does the character **do**?

Look out for and identify **action** words – **verbs** and **adverbs**. Make explicit references to what these tell us about the character.

21st

Extract from The Help. *Full text on page 104. Lines 41–42.*

Five months after the funeral, I lifted myself up out a bed. I put on my white uniform and put my little gold cross back around my neck and I went to wait on Miss Leefolt cause she just have her baby girl.

The action verbs 'lifted', 'put on' and 'went' create the impression that the character is determined and strong minded. The writer's language choices here encourage the reader to admire these qualities in the narrator, especially after the tragic death of her son.

For more about word classes, see page 19

Character through description

How does the writer **describe** the character?

21st

Extract from The Help. *Full text on page 104. Lines 15–17.*

Her face be the same shape as that red devil on the redhot candy box, pointy chin and all. Fact, her whole body be so full a sharp knobs and corners, it's no wonder she can't soothe that baby.

The narrator describes Miss Leefolt as physically awkward in appearance, with 'sharp knobs and corners', though the comparison to a 'red devil' also suggests she is quite threatening. This encourages the reader to make the link between her physical and emotional state with her inability to soothe her baby.

Look out for **describing words** and **figurative language**. Is it always the narrator who describes characters? Do other characters describe characters as well?

For more about figurative language, see page 21

Character through dialogue

What do we learn from what a character **says**?
In the extract below, Jem is talking to Dill.

Look out for the hidden aspects of a character that are revealed in dialogue.

20th

Extract from To Kill a Mockingbird. *Full text on page 102. Lines 30–38.*

Sitting down, he wasn't much higher than the collards. We stared at him until he spoke: "Hey."
"Hey yourself," said Jem pleasantly.
"I'm Charles Baker Harris," he said. "I can read."
"So what?" I said.
"I just thought you'd like to know I can read. You got anything needs readin' I can do it…."
"How old are you," asked Jem, "four-and-a-half?"
"Goin' on seven."

We learn that Dill is a show-off and an attention seeker when he immediately declares, 'I can read'. His eagerness here, however, suggests that he isn't as confident as he tries to appear. This is also hinted at when he says 'Goin' on seven', which implies he is choosing his language carefully in order to impress Jem, perhaps because he is actually quite lonely and lacking in confidence.

Remember to think about action, description and dialogue.

Now try this

Read from line 7 to the end of of **source 4**, *The Help*, on page 104. What impression do we get of the narrator's son, Treelore? Write a paragraph explaining your ideas.

Creating atmosphere

For **Paper 1**, you will need to think about how writers use a wide range of **language techniques** in order to create a particular **tone** or **mood**. Sometimes this is called the **atmosphere** of a piece of writing. You may also be asked to comment on how a writer creates a particular mood through their description of a particular **setting**.

Personification of trees – makes them seem aggressive and threatening

Metaphor comparing the drive to a ribbon and a thread, suggests drive is no longer solid or capable of carrying vehicles and 'thread' suggests it has become narrow and fragile

20th

Extract from Rebecca. *Full text on page 101. Lines 17–18.*

The drive was a ribbon now, a thread of its former self, with gravel surface gone, and choked with grass and moss. The trees had thrown out low branches, making an impediment to progress, the gnarled roots looked like skeleton claws.

Verb suggests forceful action – adds to sense of danger

Personification of drive – suggests it is literally being killed

Adjective – suggests old and decayed

Simile – creates sense of death and decay

Connotations of animal strength

Taking an overview

When you have identified the language techniques used, as well as their effects and connotations, look at whether the techniques work together to create a particular mood or tone. This is sometimes called taking an 'overview' and can help you to show the examiner that you fully understand the extract. You can also **start** with the overview: think about the mood of a text first, and then look at how it is created.

The predominant tone of the extract above is one of danger and decay.

Getting it right

You could start your answer with an overview, using phrases like these:

- Overall, the writer creates…
- The predominant tone of the extract is…

Alternatively, you could use an overview at the end of your answer, to sum up the overall effect the writer has created. You could use phrases like these:

- Subsequently, the tone created is…
- These language techniques combine to create the atmosphere of…

Now try this

Read the extract from *Rebecca*.

1 Comment on the tone created in these lines.
   - Identify as many language techniques as you can.
   - For each technique, comment on its effect or connotations.

2 Then take an 'overview'. What overall mood or tone is created by the writer?

20th

Extract from Rebecca. *Full text on page 101. Lines 20–22.*

No hand had checked their progress, and they had gone native now, rearing to monster height without a bloom, black and ugly as the nameless parasites that grew beside them.

Had a look ☐ Nearly there ☐ Nailed it! ☐

Narrative voice

For **Paper 1**, you may need to discuss **narrative voice** in your response to a question. (On rare occasions, you may also need to do this for narrative non-fiction in **Paper 2**.) Narrative voice is the 'voice' a writer of fiction chooses to tell the story. The choice of narrative voice can be used to create a particular **point of view.**

First person narrative

This is a narrative written in the **first person** and told by an **'I'**. The 'I' can be the main character or a less important character witnessing events. This point of view is effective in giving a sense of **closeness to the character** and readers are often encouraged to sympathise with them.

Extract from Rebecca. *Full text on page 101. Lines 1–4.*

Last night **I** dreamt **I** went to Manderley again. It seemed to me **I** stood by the iron gate leading to the drive, and for a while **I** could not enter, for the way was barred to **me**. There was a padlock and a chain upon the gate. **I** called in my dream to the lodge-keeper, and had no answer, and peering closer through the rusted spokes of the gate **I** saw that the lodge was uninhabited.

Third person narrative

Characters are referred to in the **third person, by their name or as 'he' and 'she'**. In a third person narrative, the narrator is not a character in the story. Sometimes this type of narrator knows everything, including a character's thoughts – this is an 'omniscient narrator', which can be used to gain the reader's sympathy; sometimes they only appear to look in from the outside.

As **she** paused at the gates, **she** shivered, feeling suddenly cold, afraid even. **She** ran her fingers lightly over the rusted lock and wondered at the rambling desolation. **She** closed **her** eyes and remembered quite clearly the house as it once was. Even then, **she** had been an outsider.

Read the second paragraph (lines 8–20) of **source 3**, *Every Man For Himself*, on page 103, then answer this **Paper 1** exam-style question:

Worked example

4 A student, having read this section of the text, commented: 'The narrator is presented as someone who can keep his head in desperate circumstances.'

To what extent do you agree?

In your response, you could:

- write about your impressions of the narrator
- evaluate how the writer has created these impressions
- support your opinions with quotations from the text.

(20 marks)

The writer has used first person narration to draw the reader into the perilous situation faced by the narrator. The focus 'I' followed by action verbs, such as 'I grabbed', 'I released', 'I choked' suggests the determination of the narrator as he focuses on the steps he is taking to survive. This brings the reader closer to the narrator and encourages sympathy for him.

✓ Clearly identifies the narrative voice.

✓ Interprets what the narrative voice suggests about the character.

✓ Suggests the effect on the reader.

Now try this

Read lines 37–45 of **source 4**, *The Help*, on page 104. Write **one** clear paragraph commenting on the writer's use of first person narration and its effects.

Remember that using a P-E-E structure can help to make your answer clear, focused and fully developed.

Putting it into practice

In **Paper 1, Section A: Reading**, you'll need to respond to **language** in a **fiction** text. Read **source 1**, *Rebecca*, on page 101. Then look at the exam-style question below and read the extracts from two students' answers.

Worked example

2 Look in detail at source 1, from **lines 5 to 16**.
How does the writer use language here to create a sense of danger and tension?
You could include the writer's choice of:

- words and phrases
- language features and techniques
- sentence forms. **(8 marks)**

In the exam, you should try to comment on sentence forms as well as vocabulary choices.

For more about sentences, see pages 31–32

Writing about language

For a question like this you should:

- ✓ spend about 10 minutes on your answer
- ✓ highlight key words in the question so that you get the focus right
- ✓ use only the lines of the text referred to in the question
- ✓ identify the language techniques used and comment on their effects.

Where you can, use the technical names for language devices in your answer. If you can't remember the specific name of the language feature, still refer to the effect created.

Sample answer extract

The writer personifies nature, which is described as having 'fingers'. This suggests that it may reach out and hurt the narrator. The writer also uses the adjective 'stealthy' to describe nature, which makes the reader feel that something hidden or secret may be lurking ahead of the narrator.

- ✗ No overview at start of answer.
- ✓ Identifies figurative device but no clear point or reference to question.
- ✓ Clearly identifies language technique and gives an example.
- ✓ Clear explanation that includes a comment about the effect on the reader.

Remember to give an overview of the mood or tone created by the language used by the writer.

Improved sample answer

Overall, the writer creates a sense of danger and tension by personifying nature as something threatening. Nature is said to have 'long, tenacious fingers', which suggests that it may actually reach out and harm the narrator. Nature is also described using the adjective 'stealthy', which makes the reader feel that something hidden or secret may be lurking ahead of the narrator.

- ✓ Very clear overview at start of answer.
- ✓ Clear quotes and explanation, which develop the point made in the overview sentence.
- ✓ Clear identification of language technique and the word 'also' signals that the point is being fully developed by using more than one piece of evidence.

Note how the points made in this answer are well developed, and how the evidence from the text is clearly explained.

Now try this

Complete the 'Improved sample answer' and aim to identify and explain **three** more relevant points.

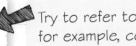

Try to refer to specific language techniques – for example, connotation, metaphor, verb.

Had a look ☐ Nearly there ☐ Nailed it! ☐

Putting it into practice

In **Paper 2, Section A: Reading**, you'll need to respond to the writer's **language choices** in a **non-fiction** text. Read **source 7a**, *On Women's Right to Vote*, on page 109. Then look at the exam-style question below and read the extracts from two students' answers.

Worked example

3 How does the writer use language to convince the audience that women should have the right to vote? **(12 marks)**

In the exam, you should try to comment on sentence forms as well as vocabulary choices.

For more about sentences, see pages 31–32

Writing about language

For a question like this you should:

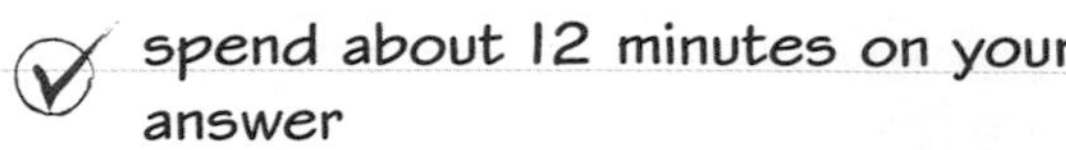

- ✓ spend about 12 minutes on your answer

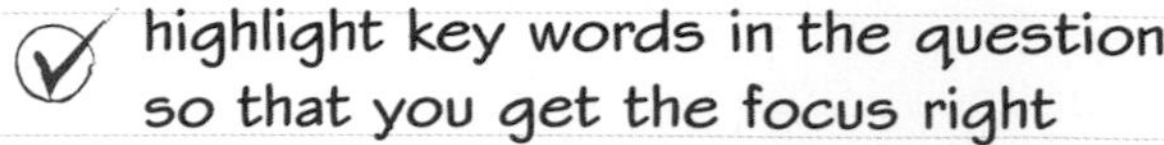

- ✓ highlight key words in the question so that you get the focus right
- ✓ refer to the whole of the source
- ✓ identify the language techniques used and comment on their effects.

Sample answer extract

The writer uses the pronoun 'we' throughout to make the reader think like she does. The fact that this is a speech in the first person also encourages her audience to agree with her. The writer also calls women 'citizens', which is about their right to have a vote.

- ✓ Clear references to language techniques and their effects.
- ✗ Clear, relevant quotations but no real explanation of their effect.
- ✗ Informal expression – needs a more precise analysis of the effect on the reader.

Remember to comment on the effect of the language on the reader.

Improved sample answer

The writer uses carefully chosen nouns and adjectives to convince her audience. For example, she describes the disqualification of women from voting as a 'violation', which carries connotations of violence as well as pointing out that it is against the Constitution. Moreover, adjectives such as 'odious' and 'hateful' highlight the strength of women's feelings towards the government, reinforcing the sense of injustice. Collectively, these techniques help to make the case that women, as 'persons', should be allowed to vote.

- ✓ Clear reference to the key points in the question.
- ✓ Effective points about the writer's choice of language techniques and their effects.
- ✓ Use of carefully selected quotations to support the points made.
- ✓ Developed explanation of the effects of the writer's language choices on the reader.

Note how this well-developed answer explains the evidence presented in support of the points made.

Now try this

Continue the 'Improved sample answer' by writing **one** paragraph of your own. Aim to identify and explain **two** more relevant points.

Try to refer to language techniques and the tone created, as well as including an overview.

Rhetorical devices 1

For **Paper 2**, you will need to think about the range of **language techniques** or **rhetorical devices** that writers use to **emphasise** their points or to **manipulate** the reader's response.

Pattern of three: a rhythmic trio of words or phrases used to highlight or exaggerate a point.

The writer has combined the ideas of the prisoner being impaired, debased and corrupted in a pattern of three in order to emphasise the sense of injustice and mistreatment suffered.

Extract from The state of the Prisons, 1818. *Full text on page 105. Line 34.*

… you return him to the world impaired in health, debased in intellect, and corrupted in principles.

Lists: a series of items or ideas, often used to highlight quantity or variety.

The writer uses a list to highlight the actions needed and to reinforce her sense of frustration at voting apathy.

Extract from 'From Suffragettes to Political Apathy'. Full text on page 110. Lines 32–34.

We need to stop our obsession with petty aspects of political leaders, and decide to ignore which politician once smoked Marijuana, or who was once was photographed eating a bacon sandwich.

Alliteration: two or more words close to each other in a sentence that begin with the same sound; often used for emphasis.

The writer uses alliteration here to draw attention to the physical and psychological damage that the prisoner is facing.

Extract from The state of the Prisons, 1818. *Full text on page 105. Lines 4–5.*

… then is he cast into the midst of a compound of all that is disgusting and depraved.

Rhetorical question: a question used to engage the reader.

This rhetorical question is used to encourage the reader to support the writer's view that prison isn't working. It also undermines the government's use of prisons and their effectiveness.

Extract from 'Prison doesn't work'. Full text on page 106. Lines 1–2.

If something didn't work 50% of the time, would you keep doing it?

Now try this

Read the final paragraph (lines 31–35) of **source 7a**, *On Women's Right to Vote*, on page 109. Identify at least **one** rhetorical device and explain its effect on the reader.

Remember to comment on the **effect** a device has, rather than just naming it. Use the technical name for the device if you know it, but even if you don't you should still comment on the language and its effect.

Had a look ☐ Nearly there ☐ Nailed it! ☐

Rhetorical devices 2

Here are some more rhetorical devices you need to be able to recognise and comment on.

Extract from Every Man For Himself. *Full text on page 103. Lines 26–28.*
The lamentations rang through the frosty air and touched the stars; my own mouth opened in a silent howl of grief. The cries went on and on, trembling, lingering – and God forgive me, but I wanted them to end.

When the narrator asks God for forgiveness for wanting the cries to end, this encourages the reader to empathise with him, particularly as he is being so honest and self-critical.

Emotive language: words intended to create an extreme response or play on the reader's emotions.

The writer uses the colloquial language of 'went on and on' to create a sense of urgency, which reflects the sense of panic.

Colloquial language: informal language used to create the impression that the writer is in conversation with the reader or to appeal to a specific audience.

The writer uses the hyperbole in 'lamentations rang through the frosty air and touched the stars' to encourage the reader to empathise with the narrator's plight.

Hyperbole: extreme exaggeration used to make a specific point, add humour or undermine an argument.

Repetition: a repeated word or phrase to emphasise an idea.

The repetition of the word 'black' is particularly effective in presenting the dark cloud that hangs over the narrator, suggesting that her sense of loss will always be repeated.

21st

Extract from The Help. *Full text on page 104. Lines 37–38.*
That was the day my whole world went black. Air look black, sun look black. I laid up in bed and stared at the black walls a my house.

Contrast: comparing two opposing or different ideas to emphasise the difference between them.

The writer contrasts the sense of a united country, which includes women, with 'male citizens' to emphasise how unjust it is that women are not allowed to vote. This is further supported by the contrast between the repetition of 'we' on one hand, and the repetition of 'male citizens' on the other.

19th

Extract from On Women's Right to Vote. *Full text on page 109. Lines 11–12.*
It was we, the people; not we, the white male citizens; nor yet we, the male citizens; but we, the whole people, who formed the Union.

Now try this

Read lines 21–28 of **source 7a**, *On Women's Right to Vote*, on page 109. Identify **two** examples of rhetorical devices. For each device, write **one** sentence about the way the writer uses it to manipulate the response of the reader.

Getting it right

Make sure you are familiar with these rhetorical devices and how they can be used:

- pattern of three
- lists
- alliteration
- rhetorical question
- colloquial language
- emotive language
- repetition
- contrast
- hyperbole

Whole text structure: fiction

Understanding the **structure** of a text is an important skill. For **Paper 1**, you will need to think about the **structure** of **fiction** texts, and how writers **organise** their writing to achieve particular **effects**.

Understanding narrative structure

When you comment on the overall structure of a fiction text, you could refer to:

Beginning–Middle–End OR Introduction–Complication–Crisis–Resolution

When you are asked to comment on structure, think about these aspects:

Structural techniques

- **Foreshadowing** (an advance sign or warning of what is to come) – for example, clues about the identity of the murderer in a crime novel
- Changes in **atmosphere** – for example, from relaxed to tense
- Changes in **characters** – could be physical or emotional
- A move from the **general** to the **specific**
- Changes in **setting**
- **Links** – between the beginning and end, between paragraphs, between characters, settings and themes
- **Different characters' perspectives** on events
- The importance of **time** – for example, links between the past and present
- **Tone** – could change from light/optimistic to dark/pessimistic

Commenting on narrative structure

Look at **source 3**, *Every Man For Himself*, on page 103. Below is an example of how you could comment on its structure.

1. And now, the moment was almost upon us…

The **introduction** in this opening paragraph is structured to generate excitement and uncertainty. The description is vague and enigmatic, heightening our interest in the events that follow.

2. As the ship staggered and tipped, a great volume of water flowed in over the submerged bows and tossed me like a cork to the roof…

The second paragraph describes the **complication**, with greater, more specific detail of the desperate situation the narrator is in. This builds up towards the crisis point in the paragraphs that follow.

3. I don't know how long I swam under that lidded sea – time had stopped with my breath – and just as it seemed as if my lungs would burst the blackness paled and I kicked to the surface…

Here, the writer presents the **crisis**. We get a real sense of the serious danger the narrator is in, particularly through the word 'blackness', which heightens the mood of uncertainty and jeopardy.

4. Gradually I grew accustomed to the darkness and made out a boat some distance away…

In the final paragraph, there is a **resolution**: the narrator has managed to survive. The use of the word 'accustomed' reinforces this, and we feel a sense of relief and admiration towards the narrator.

Now try this

Read **source 1**, *Rebecca*, on page 101. What is the link between the opening and ending paragraph?

Had a look ☐ Nearly there ☐ Nailed it! ☐

Whole text structure: non-fiction

Understanding the **structure** of a text is also important for **Paper 2**. Writers of **non-fiction** texts use structure to help present their **viewpoint** effectively.

Headings

Headings can be used to present the writer's **viewpoint.**

This headline contrasts the sacrifices of the suffragettes with the apathy of women voting today. This is an effective way of opening the argument as it provides context for the points that follow.

These are extracts from **source 7b**, 'From Suffragettes to Political Apathy'. Full text on page 110.

> From Suffragettes to Political Apathy: why it is essential that women exercise their votes

Openings

The opening or introduction needs to **engage** the attention of the reader, for example by setting the scene or introducing the main point.

This writer starts her article by providing historical context for her argument which adds authenticity and credibility to the argument that follows. By highlighting past achievements, the writer engages the reader, encouraging them to read on to discover what the situation is now.

> In 1928, after years of peaceful campaigning and militant tactics alike, a group of now-famous, inspirational women called The Suffragettes achieved their goals: women in the UK over the age of 21 were granted the right to vote.

Development

In the middle section of a non-fiction text, a writer will often provide **supporting facts** and **opinions** to encourage the reader to share their viewpoint.

Here, the writer includes facts and statistics, as well as asserting her opinion that women should be more inclined to vote. This picks up and develops the ideas in the opening, helping to build a strong, persuasive argument.

> In the 2010 Election, only 64% of women exercised their right to vote, compared to 66% of men, highlighting that although lower voter turnout is a problem facing the UK as a whole, it affects females more greatly.

Conclusion

Writers need to leave readers with a lasting impression. They can achieve this with: a direct appeal to the reader, a rhetorical question or a short, powerful statement that sums up the arguments made in the previous paragraphs.

Here, the rhetorical question and the final imperative command work together to build to an effective conclusion.

> Want to restore some of the suffragette enthusiasm for the power of politics? Register to vote in the May 2015 General Election now.

Now try this

Read **source 5a**, *The state of the Prisons, 1818*, on page 105. Write a paragraph about how the writer engages the reader in the opening section of the text.

Identifying sentence types

For **both papers** you will need to comment on the types of sentences a writer uses to **create effects** and **influence** the reader. This includes looking at the types of sentences that have been used.

Single-clause sentences

Single-clause sentences (sometimes called simple sentences) are made up of just **one clause** (a unit of information) and provide **one piece of information** about an event or action.

They contain a subject and **one verb**. For example:

I went to Manderley. — This is the verb.

Minor sentences

These are grammatically incomplete because they do not contain a verb. For example:

Our Manderley.

A labyrinth.

Surely not.

Multi-clause sentences

Multi-clause sentences (sometimes called compound and complex sentences) are made up of **more than one clause**. They contain **two or more verbs**.

Subordinate clauses

A **subordinate clause** does not make sense on its own. It is **dependent** on the main clause. For example:

The grass grew until the drive was completely covered.

This is the main clause. This is the subordinating clause.

Note how the two clauses are joined with conjunctions such as **until**, **although** and **if**. In this example, the linking word is **until**.

Sometimes, the clauses in a multi-clause sentence can be swapped round. For example:

Until the drive was completely covered, the grass grew.

Coordinate clauses

Clauses are **coordinate** if they are an **equal** pair – in other words, neither clause is dependent on the other. For example:

The gravel was gone and the grass was high.

These clauses are linked as an equal pair.

Note how the two clauses are joined with conjunctions such as **and**, **but** and **or**. In this example, the conjunction is **and**.

Now try this

What kind of sentences are these? How do you know?

1 Because the grass had grown so high, the gravel had all disappeared.
2 She stood at the gates and dreamed.
3 The house was silent.
4 Abandoned.

Commenting on sentences

How writers **structure** and **use sentences** can have just as much impact on the reader as the language they choose. This is true for **both fiction and non-fiction**.

Sentences and audience

Different sentence types can reflect a text's target reader:

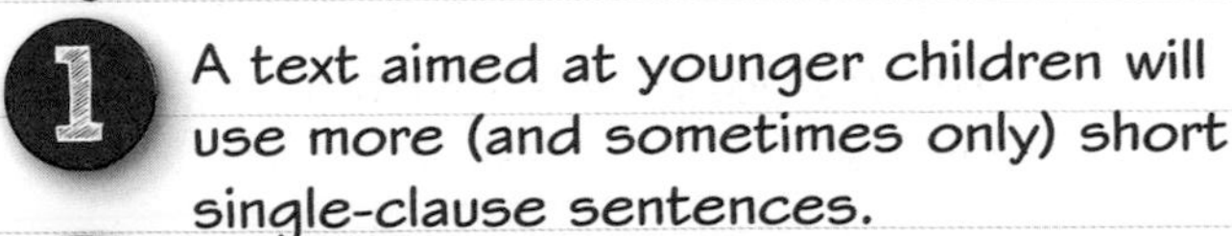

1. A text aimed at younger children will use more (and sometimes only) short, single-clause sentences.

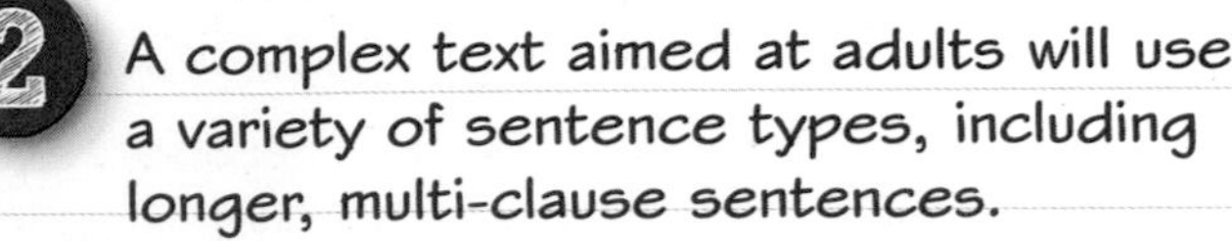

2. A complex text aimed at adults will use a variety of sentence types, including longer, multi-clause sentences.

Sentences and mood

Sentences can reflect the mood or atmosphere the writer is trying to create:

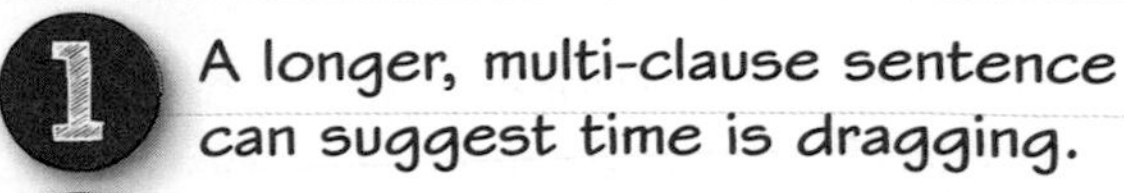

1. A longer, multi-clause sentence can suggest time is dragging.

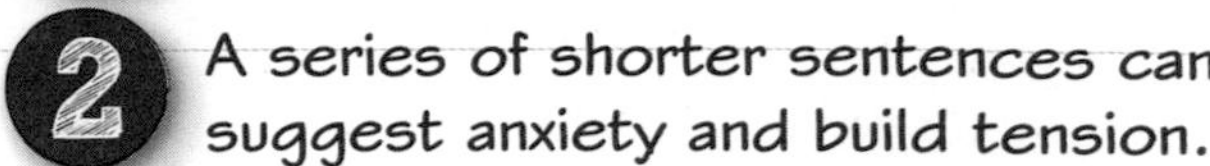

2. A series of shorter sentences can suggest anxiety and build tension.

Long and short sentences

Short, single-clause sentences can be used for dramatic effect. This can be accentuated when the short, single-clause sentence follows a longer, multi-clause sentence. Look at these examples:

Extract from The Help. *Full text on page 104. Lines 16–17.*

Fact, her whole body be so full a sharp knobs and corners, it's no wonder she can't soothe that baby. Babies like fat.

Extract from 'From Suffragettes to Political Apathy'. Full text on page 110. Lines 32–34.

We need to stop our obsession with petty aspects of political leaders, and decide to ignore which politician once smoked Marijuana, or who was once photographed eating a bacon sandwich. There are more pressing issues.

Notice how the second single-clause sentence is used for emphasis after the contrasting description in the longer, multi-clause sentence.

More about sentences

Remember that sentences can also be:

- **statements** – for example:

  She ain't gone be no beauty queen.

- **questions** or **rhetorical questions** – for example:

  If something didn't work 50% of the time, would you keep doing it?

- **exclamations** – for example:

  Dear God! Those voices!

- **commands** – for example:

  Register to vote in the May 2015 General Election now.

Think about why a writer has presented their sentences in the way they have and what effect this has.

Sentences and punctuation

Punctuation isn't just used for accuracy, although this is important. It can also be used to achieve particular effects. For example:

It? That was my first hint: something is wrong with this situation.

The use of the minor sentence and question mark reflects the narrator's shock at the way the baby is described.

For more about punctuation, see pages 91–95

Now try this

Read lines 29–36 of **source 4**, *The Help*, on page 104. Write a paragraph explaining the effect created by the writer's choice of sentence types at this point in the extract.

Putting it into practice

In **Paper 1, Section A: Reading**, you'll need to explore and comment on the **structure of** a **fiction** text. Read **source 4**, *The Help*, on page 104. Then look at the exam-style question below and read the extracts from two students' answers.

Worked example

3 Source 4 is from the opening of a novel.
How has the writer structured the text to interest you as a reader?
You could write about:

- what the writer focuses your attention on at the beginning
- how and why the writer changes this focus as the extract develops
- any other structural features that interest you.

(8 marks)

Writing about structure

For a question like this you should:

- ✓ spend about 10 minutes on your answer
- ✓ highlight key words in the question so that you get the focus right
- ✓ refer to the whole of the source
- ✓ focus on the **structure** of the text, identify the **structural devices** used and comment on their **effects**.

It isn't enough to just identify the structural technique used. You must comment on the effects of these on the reader. For example, consider what links each paragraph, whether the tone changes, and how the reader's response changes as more is revealed about characters or events.

Sample answer extract

The narrator focuses our attention on the baby because she really cared about her 'taking care a white babies' and we also learn the narrator acts like a slave because she does all the cleaning and the white people are still in bed, which isn't fair. This shows that there aren't equal rights between black and white people.

✓ Good focus on question, with accurate reference to the narrator being caring.

✗ The quotation doesn't really support the specific point made.

✗ Makes a developed point, though the expression is too conversational and descriptive, where it should be analytical.

Make sure the evidence you choose supports the point you are making. Avoid writing in a style that is too conversational or descriptive.

Improved sample answer

The narrator focuses our attention on the baby at the beginning, suggesting that she was at the centre of the narrator's world. We also get a sense of the inequality present at the time of writing, revealed when the narrator describes how she managed to support the children in everything they need 'before they mamas even get out a bed in the morning.' This links to the ideas presented later in the extract, when we discover that Mae's mother was neglectful in her attitude towards her own child, becoming reliant on and jealous of the narrator.

✓ Clear analysis of the narrative methods used.

✓ Clearly expressed contextual point that is linked to the question.

✓ Effective use of quotations to support analysis.

✓ Effective structural observations about how the opening links with other parts of the extract.

Note how this answer is much more developed, and how it makes links between the ideas presented at different points in the extracts.

Now try this

Complete the 'Improved sample answer'. Aim to identify and explain **two** more points about the structure of the source.

Had a look ☐ Nearly there ☐ Nailed it! ☐

Putting it into practice

In **Paper 2, Section A: Reading**, you **will** need to think about the **structure** of each text as part of Question 4, which asks you to compare two **non-fiction texts**.

Read **source 5b**, 'Prison doesn't work', on page 106, then look at the exam-style question and the extracts from two students' answers below. This comparison question asks students to compare two texts, but here we are focusing on how they have commented on the structure of one of the texts.

For a more detailed look at the comparison question in **Paper 2**, see pages 42–48

Worked example

4 For this question, you need to refer to the **whole of source 5a** together with **source 5b**.

Compare how the two writers convey their different attitudes to the prison system.

In your answer, you should:

- compare their different attitudes
- compare the methods they use to convey their attitudes
- support your ideas with quotations from both texts. **(16 marks)**

Writing about structure

When commenting on structure, remember to:

- ✓ explore how the writer has used structural features such as headings, the opening, the organisation of ideas, the links between ideas and paragraphs, and the conclusion
- ✓ use evidence from the text to support your analysis
- ✓ consider the effect of the structure on the reader.

For more about the structure of non-fiction texts and about comparing structure, see pages 30 and 45

Sample answer extract

The writer uses short paragraphs and subheadings to make the information in the text easier to read. The short paragraphs give the reader lots of facts and statistics about why prison doesn't work, while subheadings like 'What works better?' guide the reader through the information.

- ✓ Identifies examples of structural features.
- ✗ Relevant evidence from the text, but not fully explained.
- ✗ Limited explanation of the effect of the writer's choices on the reader, and how the structure helps the writer to convey his ideas.

Try to focus on and explain how the writer's structural choices help them to get their message across to the reader.

Improved sample answer

Leach structures his text in a way that helps him to build his argument that the prison system is ineffective. The short paragraphs used throughout the text highlight and emphasise key points in his argument, with facts and statistics to support them and persuade the reader to accept his point of view. Similarly, subheadings such as 'Not sending offenders to prison reduces reoffending by 9%' not only link each new piece of evidence to the next, but also represent his overall argument.

- ✓ A clear reference to the question, and to how the writer uses structure.
- ✓ Structural features are identified and their effects clearly analysed.
- ✓ The effects of the writer's choices on the reader and their purpose in the text are explained.
- ✓ Evidence is carefully chosen to support the point made.

Now try this

Read **source 5a**, *The state of the Prisons, 1818*, on page 105. Write **one** paragraph about how the writer's structural choices help him to present his point of view.

Evaluating a fiction text 1

Question 4 in **Paper 1, Section A: Reading** asks you to **evaluate** a text critically. This means you will need to **make a judgement** as a reader about how successful you think a particular aspect of the text is, and **explain** your thinking.

Evaluate doesn't mean you comment on whether you like or dislike a text – it is not a review!

Approaching evaluation

This will ask for your ideas about a particular aspect of the text

Focus on the aspect of the text the question is asking about – form an opinion about how successful the text is

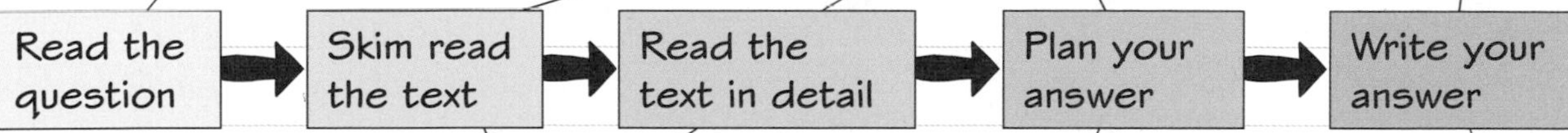

Assess the text, weighing up its strengths and weaknesses. Think about:

- the purpose of the text – what impact does the writer intend to have on the reader?
- how successful is the writer in achieving a particular effect?
- how successful is the writer in drawing you in to the text?
- alternative interpretations of the text – how might other readers respond?

For your answer:

- make a judgment as a reader – what's your personal view on the choices the writer makes and the impact this has on you?
- use your inference skills to analyse the effects of a range of the writer's choices
- explain your ideas in detail
- support your ideas with references to and quotations from the text.

To refresh your inference skills, go to page 15

Understanding an evaluation question

This exam-style question is about **source 4**, *The Help*, full text on page 104.

4 Focus this part of your answer on the first part of source 4, <u>from lines 9 to 26</u>.

A student, having read this section of the text, commented: 'In these lines, the writer is encouraging the reader to see <u>Miss Leefolt</u> in a <u>negative light</u> so that we have <u>more sympathy</u> for the <u>narrator</u>.'

<u>To what extent do you agree?</u>

In your response, you could:

- write about your own impressions of <u>Miss Leefolt and the narrator</u>
- <u>evaluate how the writer has created these impressions</u>
- <u>support your opinions with quotations from the text</u>. **(20 marks)**

Focus only on these lines of the source and only use evidence from this section.

Stick to the focus of the question.

Debate how true you feel the given view is, present an argument to support or reject it, and use evidence to support your opinion.

Present an opinion on how successful the writer is in creating these impressions, referring to the language and structural choices the writer has made.

This question is worth 20 marks, so take 2 or 3 minutes to plan your response carefully.

Now try this

Read **source 4**, *The Help*, on page 104 and consider the exam-style question above. Annotate the text with ideas that would help you to answer the question.

Had a look ☐ Nearly there ☐ Nailed it! ☐

Evaluating a fiction text 2

When you **evaluate** a text, you need to think about its **purpose** and the **effect** that the writer intends to have on the reader. Then you need to consider **how successfully** the writer manages to create this effect. Keep this in mind when you annotate the text and plan your answer.

Look at the annotated text and the extract from a student's answer below. They are both in response to the exam-style question on page 35.

Annotating a text for evaluation

21st

Extract from The Help. *Full text on page 104. Lines 13–18*

Here's something about Miss Leefolt: she not just frowning all the time, she skinny. Her legs is so spindly, she look like she done growed em last week. Twenty-three years old and she lanky as a fourteen-year-old boy. Even her hair is thin, brown, see-through. She try to tease it up, but it only make it look thinner. Her face be the same shape as that red devil on the redhot candy box, pointy chin and all. Fact, her whole body be so full a sharp knobs and corners, it's no wonder she can't soothe that baby. Babies like fat. Like to bury they face up in you armpit and go to sleep. They like big fat legs too. That I know.

- Colon starts a list of negative descriptions about Miss Leefolt, but this is the narrator talking, therefore a clearly biased viewpoint.
- Mocking tone doesn't make the narrator seem very sympathetic here.
- Comparisons of Miss Leefolt with the devil, use of colour to suggest danger – presents her in negative light which encourages the reader to dislike her.

Answering an evaluation question

Sample answer extract

The writer effectively encourages the reader to see Miss Leefolt in a negative light. This is demonstrated through the language used by the narrator to describe her, for example 'Her face be the same shape as that red devil on the redhot candy box, pointy chin and all'. This comparison with the devil and the use of colour to suggest danger encourage the reader to dislike Miss Leefolt, although I think the narrator is biased and we do not hear Miss Leefolt's version of events as the text is in the first person.

Although the impression given of Miss Leefolt is a negative one, this may not always make the reader feel sympathy for the narrator. For example, the mocking tone in phrases such as 'She try to tease it up, but it only make it look thinner' may make the reader feel she is a little unkind...

- ✓ Clear focus on the question
- ✓ Explicit references to choices made by the writer, their use of language techniques
- ✓ Relevant textual references
- ✓ A link to the effects on the reader
- ✓ Personal opinion offered

Now try this

Read **source 2**, *To Kill a Mockingbird*, on page 102. Write **one** paragraph to evaluate how the writer encourages the reader to have sympathy for Dill.

Using evidence to evaluate

When you evaluate a text, it is important to use carefully chosen, **relevant evidence** to support your ideas. Quotations can be long or short, but you must use them correctly in your answer to obtain maximum marks. The sample answer and text extracts on this page relate to *The Help*, full text on page 104.

Longer quotations

When you use a longer quotation (which runs over more than one line, for example) you should give it some space.

The reader is encouraged to view the narrator as caring and perceptive:
'*It?* That was my first hint: something is wrong with this situation.'
The rhetorical question and single word sentence encourages the reader to...

Longer quotes: what to do

1. Introduce longer quotations with a colon.
2. Start the quotation on a new line.
3. Put your quotation in quotation marks.
4. Copy your quotation accurately.
5. Start your explanation on a new line.

Shorter quotations

When you use shorter quotations you should aim to embed them in your paragraph.

The rhetorical question and single word sentence 'It?' encourage the reader to share in the narrator's disapproval and shock at Miss Leefolt's uncaring attitude towards her child.

Shorter quotes: what to do

1. You do not need to introduce each quotation with a colon or start a new line.
2. Put each quotation into quotation marks.
3. Make sure the sentence containing the embedded quotation makes sense.
4. Choose single-word quotations very carefully to ensure you can make an effective comment on them.

Shorter quotes can be more effective than longer ones. They:
- show you can identify key words and phrases
- allow you to focus on the writer's specific language choices.

Paraphrasing

Paraphrasing is when you refer closely to the text but without using a quotation. When you paraphrase, you use your own words. Paraphrase:
- when the part of the text you are referring to is too long to quote
- to avoid too many quotations 'littering' the text
- for effective summaries.

21st

Extract from The Help. *Full text on page 104. Lines 5–6.*
First day I walk in the door, there she be, red-hot and hollering with the colic, fighting that bottle like it's a rotten turnip.

You might paraphrase the extract above like this:

On the narrator's first day, the baby is ill, upset and refusing to eat.

Now try this

Read lines 1–11 from **source 4**, *The Help*, on page 104. To what extent do you agree with the view that the narrator is more experienced with children than Miss Leefolt? Write at least **one** paragraph.

Try to use quotations and paraphrasing in your answer.

Had a look ☐ Nearly there ☐ Nailed it! ☐

Putting it into practice

In **Paper 1, Section A: Reading**, you'll need to **evaluate** a **fiction** text **critically**, supported with **appropriate textual references**. Read **source 3**, *Every Man For Himself*, on page 103. Then look at the exam-style question below and read the extracts from two students' answers.

Worked example

4 Focus this part of your answer on the third paragraph of source 3, **from lines 21 to 31**.

A student, having read this section of the text, commented: 'In these lines, the writer is encouraging the reader to feel sympathy for the narrator.'

To what extent do you agree?

In your response, you could:

- write about your own impressions of the narrator
- evaluate how the writer has created these impressions
- support your opinions with quotations from the text. **(20 marks)**

Comparing writers' ideas and perspectives

For a question like this you should:

- ✓ spend about **20 minutes** on your answer, including a few minutes' **planning** time
- ✓ highlight **key words** in the **question** so that you get the focus right
- ✓ refer **only** to the **lines of the source indicated** in the question
- ✓ **critically evaluate** the text, analysing the writer's **language and structural choices** and how successful these are
- ✓ support your ideas with **relevant examples** from the source.

Sample answer extract

We are encouraged to feel the desperation of the narrator as he says the sea is black and he is trying to get air. He is scared so we are probably going to feel scared too though he wants the crying to stop which is a bit selfish.

- ✓ Focus on the question
- ✗ Paraphrasing used though the evidence doesn't directly support the point made
- ✓ Reference to effect on the reader
- ✗ Evidence of evaluation though this is undeveloped

Think about what the writer is aiming to achieve and how, and make a judgement about how successful they are in doing this.

Improved sample answer

We are encouraged to join the narrator on his desperate attempt at survival. His vivid description and hyperbolic language 'lungs would burst' and 'believed myself in hell' creates sympathy as we get a real sense of the serious danger he was in. As a reader, we also know that he must have lived to tell the tale therefore this might reduce the impact of the writing. Furthermore, when the narrator states that he wanted the cries of others to end, this is an effective way in which the writer attracts our sympathy for the narrator, as we are encouraged to admire his honesty.

- ✓ A clear focus on the question
- ✓ Reference to language choices
- ✓ A range of embedded quotations
- ✓ Explicit reference to the effect on the reader
- ✓ Evaluative style – questions the narrative style and the effect on the reader
- ✓ A developed evaluation

Remember that not all your points have to agree with the statement in the question. 'Evaluate' means to 'weigh up' and then judge. Better answers will consider alternative points of view.

Now try this

Complete the 'Improved sample answer' with **one** further evaluative point.

Writing about two texts

In **Paper 2, Section A: Reading**, two questions will ask you to refer to **both** of the **non-fiction** texts. There will be a **link** between the two texts, so they will have something in common. This will allow you to write about the **similarities and differences** between them. The questions on this page are sample questions and do not need to be answered.

One text will be from the 19th century and the other text will be from the 20th or 21st century. Remember to consider the **context** (when it was written and where it took place) as this may affect the writer's perspective.

Similarities and differences

The texts may be similar or different in various ways:

- The ideas they express about the topic.
- What they are trying to achieve (purpose).
- Their perspective (viewpoint) on the topic.
- The way they are written (language and structure).
- The effect they have on the reader.

Paper 2, Question 2

This question will ask you to refer to the whole of each source and to consider the similarities or differences (or both) between them. You will need to show your understanding by selecting information from both texts and writing about them together. This is often called **synthesis**.

synthesise *verb*
1. To combine (a number of things) into a coherent whole.
Synonyms: combine, fuse, amalgamate, build a whole

2 You need to refer to **source 6a** and **source 6b** for this question:
Use details from **both** sources. Write a summary of the differences between the experiences of Mary Seacole and Captain Scott. **(8 marks)**

This question is worth 8 marks. Focus on the key points in the question to keep your answer specific and relevant.

For more on synthesis, see pages 40–41

Paper 2, Question 4

This question also asks you to refer to the whole of each source and to consider the similarities or differences (or both) between them. You will be asked to compare the writers' ideas and perspectives.

compare *verb*
1. To examine (two or more objects, ideas, people, etc.) in order to note similarities and differences.

For more on comparing texts, see pages 44–47

4 For this question, you need to refer to the **whole of source 7a** together with **source 7b**.
Compare how the two writers convey their different attitudes towards voting.
In your answer, you should:
- compare their different attitudes
- compare the methods they use to convey their attitudes
- support your ideas with quotations from both texts. **(16 marks)**

This question is worth 16 marks. Use the bullet points to focus your answer: **'attitudes'** means **ideas and perspectives**, and **'methods'** means the **language and structural techniques** the writers use.

Now try this

Read **source 7a**, *On Women's Right to Vote*, on page 109 and **source 7b**, 'From Suffragettes to Political Apathy', on page 110. Write down **three** similarities between these two texts.

Had a look ☐ Nearly there ☐ Nailed it! ☐

Selecting evidence for synthesis

Question 2 in **Paper 2, Section A: Reading** asks you to select information from two **non-fiction texts** and **write about both texts together**. This can be challenging and the first step is to **select evidence** (information) that is relevant to the question.

This exam-style question is about **source 6a**, *Wonderful Adventures of Mrs. Seacole*, on page 107, and **source 6b**, *Captain Scott's Diary*, on page 108.

> **2** You need to refer to **source 6a** and **source 6b** for this question:
> Use details from **both** sources. Write a summary of the differences between the experiences of Mary Seacole and Captain Scott. **(8 marks)**

To find out more about skim reading, see page 7

Selecting relevant information

For this type of question, you need to select **evidence** that is **relevant** to the question:

1. **Skim read** the longer text to find the main idea of each paragraph.
2. **Identify relevant evidence.**
3. **Skim read** the second text.
4. **Identify relevant evidence** that you could combine – or **synthesise** – with the information from the first text.

First text

Here are examples of information you might select from **source 6a:**

> … I was too hard worked not to feel their effects… I cannot watch by sick-beds as I could…

Point 1: Seacole served as a nurse in the Crimean War, and helped the wounded in their 'sickbeds'.

> To be sure, I returned from it shaken in health. I came home wounded, as many others did.

Point 2: Seacole survived the Crimean War, although she returned home 'wounded'.

Second text

Here are examples of information you might select from **source 6b:**

> We camped with difficulty last night and were dreadfully cold till after our supper…

Point 1: Scott is an explorer who faces hardships on his expedition to the Antarctic, which is admirable, though the adventure was his choice.

> Monday, March 19… Amputation is the least I can hope for now, but will trouble spread? That is the serious question. The weather doesn't give us a chance…

Point 2: Scott is suffering from severe frostbite and is facing severe weather as he attempts to get back alive.

Now try this

Read the whole of **source 6a** and **source 6b**. Find **one** further difference that could be synthesised to answer the question above.

Answering a synthesis question

Once you have selected the information you need to respond to **Question 2** in **Paper 2, Section A: Reading**, you need to **synthesise** the points in your answer.

Structuring your synthesis

To **synthesise the evidence** you have selected:

1. Start with an overview that sums up your main points.

2. Write **one or two sentences for each piece of evidence** you selected.
3. Use **adverbials** to signpost the way through your synthesis.

Use key words from the question in your overview.

Linking ideas

Use adverbials like these in your synthesis to show the differences between the texts:

Both texts suggest...

However...

On the other hand...

For more about punctuation, see pages 91–95

For more about linking ideas, see page 75

This exam-style question is about **source 6a**, *Wonderful Adventures of Mrs. Seacole*, on page 107, and **source 6b**, *Captain Scott's Diary*, on page 108.

Look back at page 40, at the points selected in answer to the **Paper 2** exam-style question on the left. Then look at how they are synthesised in an extract from a student's response below.

Worked example

2 You need to refer to **source 6a** and **source 6b** for this question:
Use details from **both** sources. Write a summary of the differences between the experiences of Mary Seacole and Captain Scott.

(8 marks)

Both writers describe their experiences abroad, where their lives are at risk, but their experiences are very different. Mary Seacole is a nurse in the Crimean War, where she puts others first, looking after them in their 'sick-beds'. On the other hand, Captain Scott's expedition could be seen as more selfish: we admire his fight for survival when he is 'dreadfully cold' but it was his choice to go on this adventure.

Mary Seacole survives her experience, although she returns home 'shaken in health'; however, Captain Scott is aware he may not survive when he writes 'Amputation is the least I can hope for now'.

✓ Overview uses key words from the question, which clearly signals that the answer will be relevant.

✓ Successful and perceptive synthesis of evidence from both texts.

✓ Good choice of quotations from both texts.

✓ Effective use of adverbials and conjunctions: 'but', 'On the other hand', 'however'.

Remember to keep your answer focused on what the question is asking, and to select your evidence carefully so that it supports the points you make.

Now try this

Write **one** more synthesis paragraph about **source 6a** and **source 6b** in response to the exam-style question above. You could use the points you selected on page 40 in your answer.

Looking closely at language

Question 4 in **Paper 2, Section A: Reading** asks you to **compare** the writers' ideas and perspectives in two **non-fiction texts**. You will also need to look at the **language and structural techniques** the writers use to **convey** (put across) these ideas and perspectives.

Remember that you must not write about one text without making a comparative point about the other!

Getting it right

When comparing two texts, you should:

- establish the **meaning** and **purpose** of both texts
- identify the **specific areas of difference** between the texts
- find **specific similarities** between the texts
- give the texts **equal weighting** in your answer
- use **evidence** to support your ideas and comment on the **effect** on the reader.

Analysing the sources

Before you can answer the comparison question, you need to look **very** closely at the source texts and **question** the **language** the writer has chosen to use. You could ask yourself:

- **What is the purpose of the text?** Does the language help the text to achieve it?

The article's main purpose is to inform the reader about the problems with the prison system and to persuade them that it is not working.

- **What types and lengths of sentences has the writer used?** What effect do they have?

The writer uses short sentences for emphasis, and to draw attention to the differences in support available to different kinds of offenders.

Extract from 'Prison doesn't work', lines 1–7 and 62–66. Full text on page 106.

Prison doesn't work 50% of the time, so why do we keep sending people there?

If something didn't work 50% of the time, would you keep doing it?

One in every two criminals leaving prison will commit another crime within one year of walking out the prison gates.

If the aim of prison is to stop people committing crimes, it's not really working…

Why does prison work so badly?

… Prison reformers point to the differences between offenders leaving prison after a long time and those leaving prison after a short sentence. Offenders who leave after a longer time get more help readjusting to normal life.

Those on shorter sentences don't.

The writer's provocative viewpoint challenges the reader to rethink their view on the prison system.

The use of rhetorical questions challenges the reader to question their point of view, and support the writer's stance on prisons.

- **What tone has the writer created?** How has the writer's choice of language helped create this?

- **What techniques has the writer used?** Look out for the language techniques you revised on pages 27–28. What effect do they have in this text?

Now try this

Read the whole of **source 5b**, 'Prison doesn't work', on page 106. Identify **two** further points you could make about language. Write a sentence about each one, commenting on its effect.

Planning to compare language

Question 4 in **Paper 2, Section A: Reading** is worth **the most marks**. You will write a much better answer if you spend five minutes or so **planning** it.

Planning

Read both texts carefully and annotate them with notes about the writers' choices and the effects they create. You can then identify some similarities and differences.

Look at how one student has annotated two non-fiction texts, ready for comparison.

19th

Extract from The state of the Prisons, 1818. *Full text on page 105. Lines 1–10.*

The prisoner, after his commitment is made out, is handcuffed to a file or perhaps a dozen wretched persons in a similar situation and marched through the streets, sometimes a considerable distance, followed by a crowd of impudent and insulting boys, exposed to the gaze and to the stare of every passenger: the moment he enters prison, irons are hammered on to him; then is he cast into the midst of a compound of all that is disgusting and depraved… He may spend his days deprived of free air and wholesome exercise. He may be prohibited from following the handicraft on which the subsistence of his family depends. He may be half-starved…

- Emotive language encourages the reader to feel sympathy for the prisoner.
- Alliteration used for emphasis: 'impudent and insulting'; 'disgusting and depraved'.
- Language choices reinforce the sense of the prisoner's harsh treatment.
- Repetition is used to pile up the horrors of prison in this list, to reinforce the negative effects of prison life.

21st

Extract from 'Prison doesn't work'. Full text on page 106. Lines 2–7 and 70–74.

Prison doesn't work 50% of the time, so why do we keep sending people there?

If something didn't work 50% of the time, would you keep doing it?

One in every two criminals leaving prison will commit another crime within one year of walking out the prison gates.

If the aim of prison is to stop people committing crimes, it's not really working…

Support? You can get Job Seekers' Allowance

6 months inside is enough to mean you've lost your job, your flat and possibly your relationship. But because the sentence is comparatively short it means you don't have any support when you come out.

- Rhetorical questions challenge the reader to agree with the writer's viewpoint.
- Facts support the writer's point.
- Opinion is mingled with fact to persuade the reader to agree.
- Emotive language underlines the effects of the prison system on the prisoners.
- Pattern of three emphasises the effects of prison on prisoners' lives.

Use sentence starters like this in your comparison:
- Both texts use language to engage the reader…

Now try this

Read **source 5a**, *The state of the Prisons, 1818* (page 105) and **source 5b**, 'Prison doesn't work' (page 106). Using the student's planning notes above, write a paragraph comparing how the writers use language. Use P-E-E to structure your paragraph and remember to refer to **both** texts.

Comparing language

For **Paper 2, Section A: Reading, Question 4** you will need to look at how writers use **language** to convey their **ideas**. You will need to **compare** the language in the two texts and its **effects**.

Comparing language

When you **compare** the use of language and its effects in two texts:

- **do** make direct comparisons between language features and their effects
- **don't** simply write about the language in one text and then the language in the other text.

Extract from The state of the Prisons, 1818. *Full text on page 105. Lines 1–5.*

The prisoner, after his commitment is made out, is handcuffed to a file or perhaps a dozen wretched persons in a similar situation and marched through the streets, sometimes a considerable distance, followed by a crowd of impudent and insulting boys, exposed to the gaze and to the stare of every passenger: the moment he enters prison, irons are hammered on to him; then is he cast into the midst of a compound of all that is disgusting and depraved.

Extract from 'Prison doesn't work'. Full text on page 106. Lines 42–52.

Getting prisoners to meet their victims reduces reoffending by 14%

Campaigners for restorative justice programmes where offenders engage with the impact of their crime and often meet their victims – say it can reduce reoffending by up to 27%. A government analysis puts the improvement at a more conservative 14%. One important limitation on restorative justice is that it is only considered effective for more minor crimes such as burglary. Restorative justice isn't used for offences like domestic violence, murder or rape.

You can **either** compare similar language features in the two texts and explore their effects…

Both source 5a and source 5b use lists of negative effects to reinforce their point that the prison system needs improvement.

Or you can compare similar effects created by different language techniques.

Source 5a paints the prison system in a negative light by using emotive language to draw attention to the effect on the prisoners.

However, source 5b is more impersonal and formal. It uses facts, supported by statistics and expert evidence, to show that the prisons system is ineffective.

Now try this

Read **source 5a**, *The state of the Prisons, 1818* (page 105), and **source 5b**, 'Prison doesn't work' (page 106).

1 Identify **one** further language technique used in **both** texts.
2 Write **two** paragraphs comparing the use of language and its effects in the two sources.
3 Use an adverbial to link your paragraphs.

Comparing structure

For **Paper 2, Section A: Reading, Question 4** you will also need to look at how the writers use the **structure** of their texts to convey their **ideas**.

Comparing structure

Think about these aspects of structure. Ask yourself whether there are any similarities or differences in how the two writers use structure. What effect does this have on the reader?

Structure:
- Conclusion – the effect of the final sentences
- Heading and subheadings
- Links – between the opening and the conclusion, and between paragraphs
- Organisation of ideas – how points are sequenced
- Opening – introductory paragraph

Look at one student's notes on the openings of two non-fiction texts, and the sample comparison.

19th

Extract from On Women's Right to Vote. *Full text on page 109. Lines 1–2.*

Friends and fellow citizens: I stand before you tonight under indictment for the alleged crime of having voted at the last presidential election, without having a lawful right to vote.

Opens with engaging direct address.

Introduces main point – women's 'lawful right to vote' – and the theme of justice.

Presents herself as a 'fellow' citizen – creates sense of unity with audience.

21st

Extract from 'From Suffragettes to Political Apathy'. Full text on page 110. Lines 3–5.

In 1928, after years of peaceful campaigning and militant tactics alike, a group of now-famous, inspirational women called The Suffragettes achieved their goals: women in the UK over the age of 21 were granted the right to vote.

Opens with historical context.

Highlighting the past engages the reader – encourages them to read on.

Focus on women getting the vote sets the theme of the article.

Both writers begin by trying to encourage their audience to support the viewpoints they go on to offer. Susan Anthony opens her speech with a direct address that aims to create a sense of unity with her audience: 'friends and fellow citizens'. In this way, she encourages her listeners to support her as one of them, while also introducing the idea she develops later in the speech of women deserving equal status to men.

On the other hand, Flo Henry opens with the historical context of the fight for women's votes, encouraging the reader to read on to find out how this relates to the present day. This is used at the beginning to contrast with and highlight her later argument that women are not using their right to vote.

✓ Overview presents similarities between the texts' structures.

✓ Makes clear links between structure and the effect on the reader.

✓ Uses direct quotations and paraphrasing effectively.

✓ Links openings with rest of texts.

Now try this

Read **source 5a**, *The state of the Prisons, 1818* (page 105), and **source 5b**, 'Prison doesn't work' (page 106), focusing on the opening and final paragraphs. What is the effect on the reader of the way the writers start and finish their arguments?

Had a look ☐ Nearly there ☐ Nailed it! ☐

Comparing ideas

For **Paper 2, Section A: Reading, Question 4** you will need to compare the **ideas** that the writers present in their texts. You will need to use the **language** and **structural comparison skills** that are covered on pages 42–45 in order to do this.

4 For this question, you need to refer to the **whole of source 5a** together with **source 5b**.

Compare how the two writers convey their different attitudes to the prison system.

In your answer, you should:

- compare their different attitudes
- compare the methods they use to convey their attitudes
- support your ideas with quotations from both texts.

(16 marks)

Comparing ideas

Skim read the longer text to find the main idea of each paragraph.

Use your language and structural comparison skills (pages 42–45) to explain how the main ideas are presented.

Do the same for the shorter text.

Make it clear which text you are referring to at any time by using the name of the writer (e.g. 'Buxton suggests…') or the form of the text (e.g. 'The speech shows…').

Extract from ***source 5a*** The state of the Prisons, 1818 by Buxton. *Full text on page 105. Lines 1–5.*

The prisoner, after his commitment is made out, is handcuffed to a file or perhaps a dozen wretched persons in a similar situation and marched through the streets, sometimes a considerable distance, followed by a crowd of impudent and insulting boys, exposed to the gaze and to the stare of every passenger: the moment he enters prison, irons are hammered on to him; then is he cast into the midst of a compound of all that is disgusting and depraved.

21st

Extract from ***source 5b*** 'Prison doesn't work'. *Full text on page 106. Lines 1–11.*

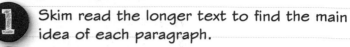

Prison doesn't work 50% of the time, so why do we keep sending people there?

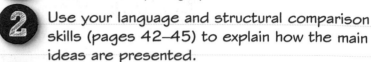

If something didn't work 50% of the time, would you keep doing it?

One in every two criminals leaving prison will commit another crime within one year of walking out the prison gates.

If the aim of prison is to stop people committing crimes, it's not really working.

- 47% of offenders leaving prison will reoffend within one year
- 58% of prisoners on short sentences reoffend within a year of leaving jail

Similarity in main idea: Both openings present a negative view of an ineffective prison system.

Similarity in language: Both writers use lists.

Difference in language and effect: Buxton's language is emotive, drawing attention to the fate of the prisoners; Leach uses statistics to highlight the ineffective system.

Similarity in structure: Both writers introduce their argument in a way that engages the reader.

Difference in structure and effect: Buxton moves from a detailed description of a prisoner's experience to a list of reasons why this is not in the law makers' 'own interest' to make the case for reform; Leach uses statistics to persuade the reader that the prison system isn't working.

Now try this

Read **source 7a** *On Women's Right to Vote* (page 109) and **source 7b** 'From Suffragettes to Political Apathy' (page 110). The main idea in both texts is that women should vote. To support this idea, find:

- **one** similarity and **one** difference in language and explain the effects
- **one** similarity and **one** difference in structure and explain the effects.

Comparing perspective

For **Paper 2, Section A: Reading, Question 4** you will need to write about the **perspective** of each writer.

Identifying perspectives

The texts in **Paper 2** will be linked. As you skim read for the main idea, identify how both writers feel about the topic. Writers often make their perspective clear at the start of their text, or sometimes at the start of the second paragraph. Here is an example of how to identify and compare perspective:

perspective *noun*
1. A particular attitude towards or way of regarding something; a point of view.
Synonyms: outlook, attitude, view, position, stand, feelings about an idea

Remember that a writer's ideas and perspectives can depend on the context in which they are writing.

19th

Extract from On Women's Right to Vote. Full text on page 109. Lines 11–16.

It was we, the people; not we, the white male citizens; nor yet we, the male citizens; but we, the whole people, who formed the Union. And we formed it, not to give the blessings of liberty, but to secure them; not to the half of ourselves and the half of our posterity, but to the whole people – women as well as men. And it is a downright mockery to talk to women of their enjoyment of the blessings of liberty while they are denied the use of the only means of securing them provided by this democratic-republican government – the ballot.

Here, the writer clearly expresses her view that women, as members of 'the whole people', should be allowed to vote.

21st

Extract from 'From Suffragettes to Political Apathy'. Full text on page 110. Lines 12–20.

In the 2010 Election, only 64% of women exercised their right to vote, compared to 66% of men, highlighting that although lower voter turnout is a problem facing the UK as a whole, it affects females more greatly. With the May 2015 General Election fast approaching… it is time to reflect on the values that these women stood for… it is vital that we exercise our right to vote, in order to challenge the dominant power structures which currently influence all of our lives. This is especially true for women.

The writer's perspective here is that not enough women are voting and that it is crucial that more of them do so.

In the opening stages of her speech, Susan Anthony feels that women, being as much part of 'the whole people' as men, should have the right to vote, whereas the suggestion in Flo Henry's article is that not enough women are exercising their hard-won 'right to vote'. To express this, Susan Anthony…

✓ This overview paragraph is used to introduce the comparison of perspectives.

✓ The words 'feels' and 'suggestion' show understanding of the writers' perspectives.

✓ Clear signposts introduce further detail.

Now try this

Read **source 7a** *On Women's Right to Vote* (page 109) and **source 7b** 'From Suffragettes to Political Apathy' (page 110). Do the writers keep the same perspective throughout or do they end with a different point of view? Explain your answer.

You will need to write about structure, too, so remember to look at differences between the beginning and end of texts.

Had a look ☐ Nearly there ☐ Nailed it! ☐

Answering a comparison question

Writing about and **comparing two texts** for **Paper 2** can be challenging unless you structure your answer carefully. To make your answer clear to an examiner and to fully show your understanding, you need to use an **effective structure** for your answer.

Structure

Aim to make direct comparisons.

You could **focus on one language or structural feature** or its effect in the first text, then compare it to a similar feature or effect in the second text.

You could also compare how the writers make **different choices** to achieve **similar effects**. For example, you could write about how the writers use language to create different tones in the two texts but which help both writers to make their point.

Linking words and phrases

Use adverbials to signpost the way through your answer.

For example, you could **signpost a similarity** using adverbials such as: 'Similarly...' or 'In the same way...'

To **signpost a difference**, you can use adverbials such as: 'However...' or 'On the other hand...'

Worked example

Write a brief overview in **one** sentence summarising the two texts and their purposes.

Both texts are about... but **source** A aims to... while **source** B tries to...

Write about a language or structural feature in **source A**, supported with evidence and an explanation of its effect on the reader.

Source A uses...

Similarly, **source** B uses...

Use an adverbial to link a point about a similar language or structural feature in **source B**. Support this with evidence and explanation as well.

Both texts use emotive language. For example, **source** A...

This makes the reader realise that...

On the other hand, **source** B uses emotive language to achieve a different effect...

The writer has created a humorous tone in **source** A. He has done this by using puns such as...

However, the writer of **source** B has created a much more disturbing tone by...

Both writers use rhetorical questions though for a different purpose...

The emotive language in **source** A is intended to gain sympathy for the narrator, whereas it is used in **source** B to reinforce the sense of injustice...

Now try this

Use the structure in the worked example above to write the **first paragraph** of an answer to Question 4 on page 46.

Remember to spend a couple of minutes planning before you start to write.

Getting it right

Remember that you need to compare the writers' ideas and perspectives (attitudes), as well as how these are conveyed. You need to think about the language and structure the writers have used and what effect these have on the reader. Focus on the question. Are you being asked to compare similarities or differences, or both? Make sure your answer is focused on the question and remember to support your ideas with quotations from both texts.

Putting it into practice

In **Paper 2, Section A: Reading**, you'll need to **compare** the writers' **ideas and perspectives**, and how they are presented, in **two non-fiction texts**. Read **source 7a**, *On Women's Right to Vote*, on page 109, and **source 7b**, 'From Suffragettes to Political Apathy', on page 110. Then look at the exam-style question below and read the extracts from two students' answers.

Worked example

4 For this question, you need to refer to the **whole of source 7a** together with **source 7b**.

Compare how the two writers convey their different attitudes to rights and responsibilities.

In your answer, you should:

- compare their different attitudes
- compare the methods they use to convey their attitudes
- support your ideas with quotations from both texts. **(16 marks)**

Comparing writers' ideas and perspectives

For a question like this you should:

- ✓ spend about **20 minutes** on your answer, including **5 minutes planning**
- ✓ highlight **key words** in the **question** so that you get the focus right
- ✓ refer to the **whole** of **both sources**
- ✓ identify the **language** and **structural devices** used and comment on their effect on the reader.

Sample answer extract

Flo Henry thinks women should take responsibility and calls suffragettes 'inspirational' to make her point, whereas Susan Anthony says that women are her 'friends and fellow citizens'. Flo Henry also thinks that women should use their rights more and says '22.7% of women make up parliament', which shows that women don't have the same rights as men. Susan Anthony doesn't use facts though she does use the rhetorical question 'Are women persons?', which suggests they don't have rights.

✗ A focus on the key words in the question, though no overview given.

✓ Specific references to both writers.

✗ Reference to a language technique, but the explanation of its effect is limited.

✗ Use of quotations, though these don't always support the point directly.

Remember to structure your answer so that the links between your points, evidence and explanations are clear.

Improved sample answer

Both writers explore rights and responsibilities, though from different perspectives. Anthony believes the government should provide women's rights, whereas Henry argues that women are irresponsible by not using their right to vote. Anthony is more personal and direct in her criticism of the government, using the repetition in 'this government is not a democracy. It is not a republic. It is an odious aristocracy' to highlight her feelings of injustice; on the other hand, Henry's viewpoint, as a journalist, is less emotive, presumably because she is not as directly affected by events as Susan Anthony.

✓ Overview gives a clear sense of the subtle differences in viewpoints expressed.

✓ Explicit reference to the writers' choices and their impact.

✓ Aptly chosen quotations support the observations made.

✓ Relevant contextual observation supports the comparison.

✓ Comment on the effect on reader.

Now try this

Complete the 'Improved sample answer' with at least **one** more paragraph. Try to pick up on both similarities and differences in the language and structure.

Had a look ☐ Nearly there ☐ Nailed it! ☐

Writing questions: an overview

Both papers of the English Language GCSE include a **Writing** section (Section B). There are different types of writing task in each paper.

Paper 1, Section B: Writing

Paper 1 tests your skills in **descriptive or narrative writing.**

Creative writing → Write **one** text **from a choice of two** tasks

The writing tasks will be linked by a topic to the reading texts in Paper 1, Section A: Reading.

- One of the tasks will have a visual stimulus to help you with ideas.
- This section is worth 40 marks (50% of Paper 1).

Paper 2, Section B: Writing

Paper 2 tests your skills in **writing to present a viewpoint.**

Viewpoints and perspectives → Answer **one question. There is no choice of task.**

The writing tasks will be linked by a theme to the reading texts in Paper 2, Section A: Reading.

- You will write for a specific audience and purpose, and in a specific form.
- This section is worth 40 marks (50% of Paper 2).

Find out more about the reading texts on pages 3–4

Assessment objectives

Assessment objectives are the **skills** you are tested on in the exam questions. For writing, the assessment objectives are the same for both papers.

You need to remember what skills you will be tested on for each paper. The exam papers will not remind you.

Assessment objective 5

- Communicate clearly, effectively, and imaginatively, selecting and adapting tone, style and register for different forms, purposes and audiences.
  - Express your ideas clearly and fluently.
  - Be original and imaginative in your ideas.
  - Choose the right form for your writing.
  - Use the most appropriate language for your audience.
- Organise information and ideas, using structural and grammatical features to support coherence and cohesion of texts.
  - Plan and structure your work, using sentences and paragraphs effectively.
  - Use adverbials and other devices to link your ideas together effectively.

AO5 is worth 24 marks (60%) of each Writing answer.

Assessment objective 6

Use a range of vocabulary and sentence structures for clarity, purpose and effect, with accurate spelling and punctuation.

- Vary the length and types of sentence you use.
- Spell and punctuate correctly.
- Use interesting and effective words.

AO6 is worth 16 marks (40%) of each Writing answer.

Now try this

Answer the following questions using the information on this page.

1 The questions in one paper require you to write about your own point of view. Which paper is this?
2 How many writing questions do you need to answer for each paper?
3 Which paper or papers will require you to vary the length and type of your sentences?

Writing questions: Paper 1

Paper 1, Section B: Writing will test the quality of your skills in **descriptive or narrative writing**.

Descriptive writing

descriptive writing *noun*
1. painting a picture with words in a way that entertains your reader.

To write a description:

- write in paragraphs
- use a range of sentence structures and vocabulary choices to engage your reader
- focus on creating atmosphere, rather than plot.

Narrative writing

narrative writing *noun*
1. the process of expressing a sequence of events.

To write a narrative you need to structure your writing carefully, usually with a clear beginning, middle and end.

Getting it right

- Decide which question you are going to answer as quickly as you can – which do you have the most ideas about?
- Read the question carefully.
- Identify the purpose, audience and form of the writing.

Identifying purpose, audience and form

These are examples of the two types of questions you will find in the exam.

5 You are going to enter a creative writing competition.
Your entry will be judged by a panel of people of your own age.
Either:
Write a description suggested by this picture:

Or:
Write the opening part of a story about a character who wants to turn back time.
(40 marks)

Purpose and audience – Look for clues about the purpose and audience. In this example, the answers to both questions would need to be imaginative, engaging and suitable for students your own age.

Form – Look out for where the form is given in the question. For Paper 1 you will need to write a description or a narrative.

In the exam you might find:

- a choice of description or narrative tasks
- a choice of two description tasks
- a choice of two narrative tasks.

Watch out for any details relating to form.
In the second option, you only need to write the opening of a story – not the whole story!

Now try this

Look at the **Paper 1** exam-style question below. Annotate the question to identify the purpose, audience and form. Then jot down as many ideas as you can.

5 Your school is running a creative writing competition.
Your entry will be judged by a panel of students from your own year group.
Write the opening part of a story about a child during wartime. **(40 marks)**

Had a look ☐ Nearly there ☐ Nailed it! ☐

Writing question: Paper 2

Paper 2, Section B: Writing will test the quality of your skills in **writing to present a viewpoint**.

Writing to present a viewpoint

viewpoint *noun*
1. a writer's attitude and opinion on a particular subject.

When you are writing to present a point of view, you may need to write in a way that argues, explains, persuades or informs, for example.

What you write does not need to be based on a real, personal opinion. You can make up your viewpoint.

Getting it right

- Read the question carefully.
- Identify the purpose, audience and form of the writing.
- Organise your ideas to create an impact on the audience.

There is only one writing question in Paper 2. You will not have a choice of questions.

Identifying purpose, audience and form

This is an example of the type of question you will find in the exam.

> **5** 'Social networking is making teenagers anti-social.'
> Write an article for a teen website in which you argue for or against this statement. **(40 marks)**

This statement presents a particular point of view. You will need to write from your own viewpoint (real or imagined) on the topic.

The writing tasks will be linked by theme to the reading texts in Paper 2, Section A: Reading. You may wish to use these texts as a way of generating ideas.

Form – This clearly tells you what form your writing must take. Here, it is an article. You will need to include features of this form in your writing.

Purpose – Look out for the purpose of the writing. The main purpose is to present your viewpoint. To do this, you may need to argue, explain, persuade or inform, or a combination of these.

Audience – For Paper 2, the audience will be clear in the question. Here, the audience is teenagers. Keep your audience in mind as you plan and write your response.

Generating ideas

One of the best ways of generating ideas is to consider who is affected by the topic you are writing about. Look at the student's notes opposite. They are about the exam-style question above.

Who is affected by this?
- Teenagers – social networking makes them less confident face to face
- Parents – can cause conflict and affect relationships within a family...
- Teachers – students could be tired and lack motivation

Now try this

Look at the **Paper 2** exam-style question below. Annotate the question to identify the purpose, audience and form. Then jot down as many ideas as you can.

> **5** 'Mobile phones should be banned from schools because they cause a distraction during lessons.'
> Write a letter to the headteacher at your school in which you argue for or against this statement. **(40 marks)**

Writing questions: time management

Managing your time effectively as you answer the writing questions on **both papers** is very important.

How long to spend writing

You could spend a total of 45 minutes on each Writing section. For example:

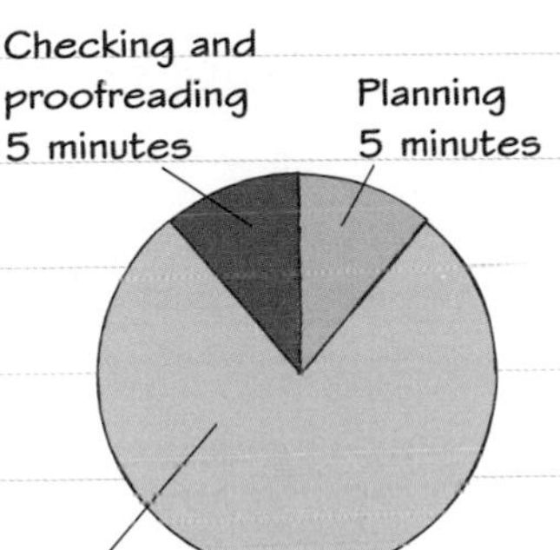

Turn to page 99 for more about proofreading

Getting it right

The Writing sections are at the end of each paper. Make sure you don't spend too long on Section A: Reading; otherwise you may run out of time to finish answering the writing tasks.

Find out more about planning your overall time in the exam on page 2

Coming up for air

As you write, pause regularly. Take a deep breath, have a drink of water and check your answer is still focused on the question. Ask yourself:

- Am I still writing in the correct form?
- Will my target reader be engaged by this?
- Am I achieving my purpose?
- Am I making a range of points or repeating myself?
- Should I move on to my next point now?
- How much time have I got left?

Running out of time

You may not have time to include all the ideas from your plan in your answer. If this happens:

- **Don't** panic!
- **Don't** stop half-way through a sentence.
- **Try** to express your remaining ideas more concisely.
- **Take out** some of your ideas if they are very similar to points you've already made.
- **Include** a conclusion/final paragraph – as you are assessed on your ability to structure your writing, including the ending.

Finishing under time pressure: an example

5 'Supporting local sport is important for the community. It is the responsibility of local businesses to make sure adequate funding is available.'
Write a letter to the local council in which you explain your point of view on this statement.
(40 marks)

Problem: You only have time for one more paragraph but you still haven't covered these points from your plan:
- Benefits to the community
- Personal stories about my football team
- Conclusion

Recently, my football team have been running training sessions for local primary school students on a voluntary basis. This kind of charitable work is vital in reaching out to children who might not otherwise have access to this kind of experience, and in promoting a healthy, active lifestyle.

Strategy: Combine these items by providing a personal example of how the community has benefitted from your football team.
- Saves time
- Makes your writing more fluent and concise
- Gets straight to the point, which fits purpose and audience

Now try this

Rewrite the key advice points from this page as a tweet. Remember: you only have 140 characters!

Writing for a purpose: creative 1

For **Paper 1**, whether you're writing a narrative or a description, you will almost certainly want to include descriptive elements to engage your reader. There are a number of **descriptive techniques** you can use to help you.

The five senses

When you write to describe a place or an experience, you want the reader to experience what it was like to *be* there.

The only way we can experience anything is through our senses:

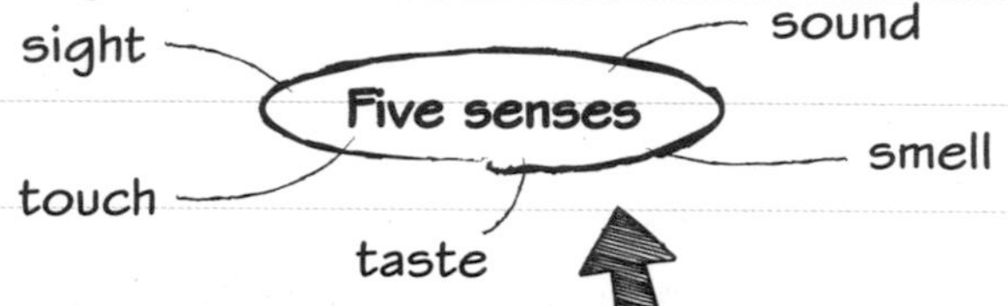

Often writers focus on the sense of sight. By using the other four senses as well, you can create **much** more vivid descriptions.

Figurative language

Figurative language, or **imagery**, can create an image in the reader's mind. It includes devices such as:

- similies
- metaphors
- personification.

Used sparingly and imaginatively, figurative language can help to create rich and powerful descriptions.

Remember to avoid clichés (well-known, overused figurative language). Describing someone as 'cool as a cucumber' or a landscape as 'flat as a pancake' does not demonstrate imagination and originality.

Feelings

Describing the narrator's feelings can bring descriptive writing to life. It helps the reader understand and share those feelings. Remember to **show** the reader how the narrator feels, rather than **tell** them. For example, it is much more effective to write:

> A smile spread across my face and warm satisfaction rose from my stomach to the tips of my ears.

than:

> I felt really, really happy.

Language choice

In descriptive writing, it can be tempting to use as much descriptive language as possible. It's much more effective to use fewer words which you have chosen really carefully. Try to use one precise descriptive word, rather than three vague words. For example:

> I danced across the road

creates a much more immediate and powerful picture than:

> I walked cheerfully with a spring in my step across the road as though I were dancing.

Think about the **quality** of your descriptive language, not the **quantity**.

Now try this

Write the first paragraph of your response to this **Paper 1** exam-style question. Try to use some of the techniques on this page.

> **5** Your school magazine is asking for examples of creative writing for the next edition. Describe an occasion when you were frightened. **(40 marks)**

Writing for a purpose: creative 2

If you write a narrative for **Paper 1**, there are a number of **narrative elements** to consider.

Narrative voice

Unless the exam paper tells you which narrative voice to use, you can choose for yourself. Remember:

- a **first person narration** can give the reader a **sense of closeness to the narrator**
- a **third person narrator** can be **omniscient** – knowing the thoughts and feelings of all characters
- you must stick to the narrative voice you choose throughout your answer!

Turn to pages 24 and 66 for more on narrative voice and structure

Engaging the reader

As with descriptive writing, you can use these techniques to draw the reader in:

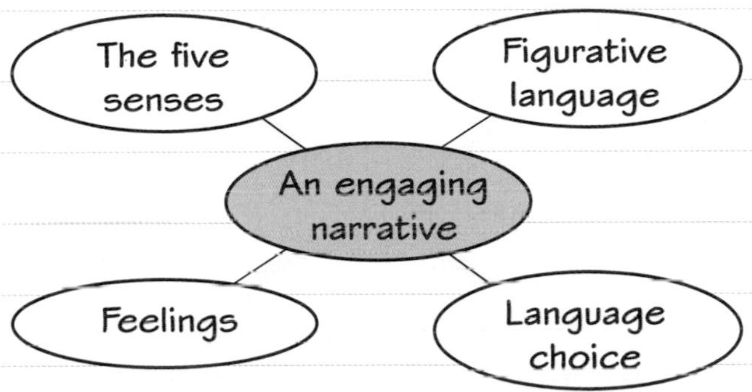

Turn to page 54 for a reminder about techniques to engage the reader

Structure

- Structure your writing carefully.
- Unless the question tells you otherwise (for example, if you are only asked to write a story opening), your writing should have a clear beginning, middle and end.
- Don't provide all the answers in the first paragraph – engage the reader with hints of what's to come.

Things to avoid

- Too much plot or action – focus on the key dramatic moments.
- Describing events that are unimportant.
- Too many characters or places – your reader won't have time to process a range of complex relationships between characters, so keep it simple.

Worked example

5 You are going to enter a creative writing competition. Your entry will be judged by a panel of people your own age.
Write the opening of a story about someone who overcomes their fears. **(40 marks)**

Matthew, the frail teenager who still lived with that dark secret, shivered incessantly in the damp, cold church, like a prisoner awaiting execution. Loneliness, he was used to, but this sight that lay in front of him, was something that even his father hadn't prepared him for.

✓ Unusual adjective 'frail' to describe a teenager, provides an engaging opening.

✓ Hints at disturbing past are used to engage the reader.

✓ Powerful verbs and adverbs create a sense of danger.

✓ Setting of the church and the bleak simile add mystery and intrigue.

✓ Use of the senses draws the reader into the scene.

Now try this

Reread the student's opening paragraph above. Then write the next paragraph. Keep the question in mind as you write. Try to use some of the techniques on this page.

Had a look ☐ Nearly there ☐ Nailed it! ☐

Writing for a purpose: viewpoint 1

For **Paper 2** you need to write to present your **viewpoint**. For example, you may have to **argue** your point of view and/or **persuade** the reader to agree with you. Remember that you can adopt a persona before expressing your point of view – it doesn't have to be your own personal viewpoint.

Key points

The power of your argument or persuasion relies on the strength of your key points.

To argue your viewpoint, choose key points which highlight:

- why you are right
- why those who disagree are wrong.

To persuade, choose key points which highlight:

- what is **wrong** with the way things are
- how your ideas will make things **better**.

Evidence

Always support **each** of your key points with convincing evidence. For example:

- facts or statistics
- an expert opinion
- an example from your own experience.

Linking ideas

Use adverbials to signpost the path your argument is going to follow.

To build your argument:

- furthermore...
- additionally/In addition...
- moreover...

To introduce counter-arguments:

- however...
- on the other hand...

To explain and develop your points:

- consequently/as a consequence...
- therefore...

Turn to pages 75–76 for more about adverbials.
See pages 27–28 for more on rhetorical devices.
Find out more about direct address on page 83

Counter-arguments

Think about how your reader might disagree with you. Then point out why they are wrong. This is called making a 'counter-argument' and is an effective way of dealing with opposing ideas. For example:

> Some people think that teenagers are lazy and uncaring. However, it is the media who give us these negative images by ignoring all the teenagers who work hard, behave responsibly and raise money for charity.

Remember to use adverbials to show that you are dismissing an opposing view.

Rhetorical devices

To engage your reader and add power to your argument or persuasive writing, use:

- rhetorical questions
- direct address
- repetition
- lists
- alliteration
- contrast
- pattern of three
- emotive language
- hyperbole.

Now try this

Aim to:

- note down three key points, supported by evidence
- make a counter-argument
- write three sentences using three different rhetorical devices.

Note down some ideas you could use in your response to the **Paper 2** exam-style question below:

5 'Talent shows are a terrible idea. They encourage ruthless competition and they allow the talentless to make fools of themselves.'

Write an article for your school magazine in which you explain your point of view on this statement.

(40 marks)

Writing for a purpose: viewpoint 2

For **Paper 2** you need to write to present your **viewpoint**. You may need to **inform** or **explain** something to the reader to help you get your point of view across.

When you present a **viewpoint**, you may need to argue/persuade and inform/explain in the same text! Rhetorical devices are important in arguments, so always make sure you choose language that is appropriate for **purpose** as well as **audience**.

Techniques to inform and explain

Facts and statistics

These suggest the information in a text can be trusted. You can make facts and statistics up, but they need to be believable.

You may be able to use facts and statistics from the source texts in Section A: Reading to help you.

Language

Writing that informs and explains is often **factual**, so you should usually avoid figurative language and rhetorical devices.

Adverbials

Use adverbials to guide the reader through the information. When you write to inform or explain you may need to use **temporal (time) adverbials** such as **first**, **then**, **next** and **finally**.

Register

A formal register suggests the information is unbiased and reliable. Use formal language and standard English.

For more about register, see pages 77–78

Presenting a viewpoint

Presenting a point of view can combine different types of writing:

... I am confident you will agree that the curfew would prevent teenagers participating in sport, prevent them attending invaluable study groups and, indeed, prevent them leading active, healthy social lives. While it may be true that a small number of teenagers cause trouble during the evening hours, it is inexcusable to penalise all teenagers as a result. Firstly, young people need the opportunity to form strong friendships and support networks, and for 75% of teenagers these vital bonds are formed outside school...

Argue and persuade

Rhetorical devices (direct address, repetition, pattern of three) to engage the reader

Counter-argument to deal with opposing ideas

Inform and explain

Temporal adverbial to guide the reader

Factual detail to inform

Statistics to suggest the information is trustworthy

Explanation of why the curfew is bad for teenagers

Now try this

Look at this **Paper 2** exam-style question opposite.

1 Write a sentence describing the register you would use in this task, and how you would achieve it.

2 Write down any facts or statistics you could include in your writing.

3 Write the **first two** sentences of your answer.

5 'Being a teenager in the modern world is difficult and parents should help them by being understanding and supportive.'
Write an article for a magazine aimed at parents in which you explain your point of view on this statement. **(40 marks)**

Had a look ☐ Nearly there ☐ Nailed it! ☐

Writing for an audience

The writing tasks will usually tell you the audience you are writing for. You need to make your writing appealing, appropriate and accessible **to that audience.**

Identifying the audience

In some questions, the audience (person or people) you are writing for may be clearly **stated**:

> **5** Write a letter to your local MP... **(40 marks)**

Your writing **must address** an adult (the MP) and will require a formal response.

Other questions may imply (hint at) an audience:

> **5** Write an article for your local newspaper... **(40 marks)**

Think carefully about **who** would read this type of newspaper – in this case, it will probably be adults but may include teenagers.

Writing for an adult audience

When writing for an adult audience, you will usually need to write in a formal style and use standard English. Avoid non-standard English, including: texting language (e.g. LOL); slang (e.g. I was gutted); double negatives (e.g. I ain't never done that).

For more about formality and standard English, see pages 77–78

Writing for a teenage audience

When writing for a teenage audience, you should still avoid non-standard English. However, some carefully used informal language may be an appropriate way to engage the audience.

Both these answers give the same information. However, notice how informal language has been carefully mixed with more formal language to engage the teenage audience.

Worked example

5 'It is the parents' responsibility to ensure their children meet homework deadlines.'
Write a speech aimed at parents... **(40 marks)**

Parents have a vital role in helping their children meet homework deadlines. Many teenagers, when a deadline has been missed, have a tendency to avoid dealing with the situation. Your role is to encourage them to speak to their teachers and ask for the help that is available at school.

Worked example

5 'Homework and homework deadlines are a frequent cause of stress in teenagers.'
Write a speech for a Year 11 assembly... **(40 marks)**

Let's get things straight. Homework is a pain... and that's putting it mildly. We can all think of much better ways to occupy our time, and frequently many of us do just that! However, if you are behind with your homework, speak to your teacher as soon as you can. After all, they are there to help.

✓ The speech begins with informal figurative language that is appropriate to engage the audience. It is then developed using carefully crafted, more formal language.

Now try this

Rewrite the opening paragraph of the student answer below, using formal standard English that is more appropriate to the audience.

5 'Exams are important and students should prepare for them carefully.'
Write an article for your school website ... **(40 marks)**

You reckon you've got ages until your GCSEs? You've already bagged a job? I'm telling you, those exams are coming round quick!

This answer is far too informal. The text should be appropriate for students and parents – and formal enough to suggest the information is reliable.

Putting it into practice

In **Paper 1, Section B: Writing**, you'll need to use your skills in **descriptive or narrative writing**. Before you start writing, you should think carefully about the question options.

Here is one student's exam plan for the Paper 1 writing question. Fill in the gaps.

Timing
Planning:
Writing: 35 mins (10.05–10.40)
Checking:

For a reminder about the structure of Paper 1, Section B: Writing, go to page 51

Preparing for creative writing

You should:

- plan your time – you have about **45 minutes** for this question, including planning and checking

- read the **question options** carefully

- decide **which question** to answer
- **plan** your writing, including ideas about narrative or descriptive techniques.

Look carefully at the question options. Think about what each option might involve before you decide which one to answer. Look at this student's thoughts:

The purpose is clear – I need to make my writing as engaging as possible.

The audience is students my own age – my writing will need to appeal to them.

I can either write a description or a narrative – for the narrative, I only need to write the opening of the story.

Neither option specifies a narrative voice, so I can choose which narrative voice to write in, e.g. first or third person.

The image in the first option could help me with ideas.

5 A national newspaper is running a creative writing competition.

Your entry will be judged by a panel of students your own age.

Either:

Write a description suggested by this picture:

Or:

Write the opening part of a story about a deserted house. **(40 marks)**

Now try this

Look closely at the **Paper 1** exam-style question below. You do not need to write an answer. Instead:

- plan your time as if you were in the exam
- read the question carefully, making notes about purpose, audience, form and narrative voice
- use a spider diagram or bullet points to get down your initial ideas.

5 The English department at your school is asking for examples of creative writing for a wall display. Describe an occasion when you met a mysterious person. **(40 marks)**

Had a look ☐ Nearly there ☐ Nailed it! ☐

Putting it into practice

In **Paper 2, Section B: Writing**, you'll need to use your skills in **writing to present a viewpoint**. Before you start writing, you should think carefully about the question and plan your time.

Here is one student's exam plan for this section. Add the missing details.

Timing
Plan: 5 mins (10.00–10.05)
Write:
Check:

For a reminder about the structure of Paper 2, Section B: Writing, go to page 52

Preparing to present a viewpoint

You should:

- plan your time – you have about **45 minutes** to answer the question, including planning and checking
- read the **question** carefully
- **annotate** the question to highlight the **purpose, audience and form**
- **plan** your answer.

Look carefully at the question and identify exactly what you are being asked to do. Look at how this student has annotated the key features of this question:

This statement presents a particular point of view. I need to write about my own point of view.

My writing needs to take the form of a letter. The letter will need to be formal, as it's to the local paper.

The audience is the newspaper, but I need to think about who will read the paper – it will mainly be adults but some teenagers may read a local paper, too.

I need to decide on my point of view, whether I agree with the statement or not, then argue my case.

For Paper 2, you will not be able to choose which question to answer. There will only be one option and you will need to answer that.

5 'At 17, teenagers are too irresponsible to drive. The minimum age to drive a car should be raised to 21 years.'
Write a letter to your local newspaper in which you argue for or against this statement.
(40 marks)

Now try this

Look closely at this **Paper 2** exam-style question. You do not need to answer the question. Instead, draw a four-point spider diagram to identify the purpose, audience, form and your own point of view about the statement.

5 'British beaches are filthy. It will take a community effort to clean them up and keep them clean.'
Write an article for a broadsheet newspaper in which you explain your point of view on this statement.
(40 marks)

Form: articles

The writing question in **Paper 2** may ask you to write an article.

The headline gives enough information to intrigue the reader – and may use a pun, alliteration, repetition, rhetorical question, etc.

The subheading gives more information, drawing the reader in.

You don't need to be a talented artist – a box with a brief description of the image will do. You are not marked on your drawing ability!

The truth about lying: it's the hands that betray you, not the eyes

By analysing videos of liars, the team found there was no link to their eye movements

ADAM SHERWIN

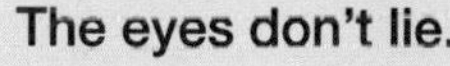

The eyes don't lie.

It is often claimed that even the most stone-faced liar will be betrayed by an unwitting eye movement.

But new research suggests that "lying eyes", which no fibber can avoid revealing, are actually a myth.

Verbal hesitations and excessive hand gestures may prove a better guide to whether a person is telling untruths, according to research conducted by Professor Richard Wiseman.

Many psychologists believe that when a person looks up to their right they are likely to be telling a lie. Glancing up to the left, on the other hand, is said to indicate honesty.

But the experts are wrong, according to Prof Wiseman, a psychologist from the University of Hertfordshire: 'The results of the first study revealed no relationship between lying and eye movements, and …'

In the exam, you don't have to write your headline in bold block writing. Your normal handwriting will do.

Opening paragraphs summarise the key points to engage the reader.

Later paragraphs add more detail.

Quotations from experts or people involved in the story add interest and authenticity. Note how speech punctuation is used correctly.

Now try this

Look at this **Paper 2** exam-style question. Write the first **three** paragraphs of your article. Try to:

- sum up your key ideas in paragraph 1
- add more detail in paragraph 2
- use a quotation in paragraph 3.

5 'Talent shows are a terrible idea. They encourage ruthless competition and they allow the talentless to make fools of themselves.'

Write an article for your school magazine in which you explain your point of view on this statement. **(40 marks)**

Form: letters and reports

For **Paper 2**, you may be asked to write a letter or report.

Letters

Your address and the date go in the top right-hand corner. You don't have to write your real address.

The person you are writing to and their address goes on the left, lower down.

Use 'Dear Sir/Madam' if you don't know the name of the person.

Use **Yours faithfully** if you have used 'Dear Sir/Madam'. If you have used the person's name, end with **Yours sincerely.**

'Yours' has a capital letter, but '**sincerely**' and '**faithfully**' do not.

57 Woodford Road
Nottingham NG8 4PQ

16 February 2015

The Editor
Nottingham News
17 High Street
Nottingham
NG2 4XY

Dear Sir/Madam

It has come to my attention...

and hope that you will take this into account.

Yours faithfully

Jane Smith

Getting it right

In the exam, the most important thing is the quality of your writing. Indicate that it is a letter you are writing – for example, by using 'Dear...' at the start – but make sure your focus is on the tone and content of your writing.

Reports

Title – This should be formal and factual.

Introduction – Two or three sentences giving the main facts about the topic.

Current situation – This says what is happening now.

Recommendation – This gives an idea about what should change.

Conclusion – This summarises what advantages the proposed change will bring.

Reports are information texts and should be formal and factual, but you will probably need to give your opinions as part of the recommendations you make.

School Marathon Events

Most major cities across the world hold marathon events. These events collect thousands of pounds in sponsorship for charities, from the large, well-known national organisations to small, local ones that are personal to the runners.

Our school currently takes part in national events such as Comic Relief and Children in Need. Such events provide the school with an engaging vehicle for teaching a variety of subjects in a way that engages students of all ages. Last year... However, whilst they are well supported within the school they do not involve the wider community.

A school marathon would create an ideal opportunity to reach out...

So a school marathon event would combine two factors that are essential to a well-rounded education: physical activity and the promotion of empathy.

Go back to page 57 for more about informative writing

Now try this

Look at the letter and report on this page. Which form would be most suitable for the following tasks?

1 An application to join the Royal Air Force.
2 A proposal to install new fitness equipment in the school gym.
3 A thank you to your elderly grandparents for the present they sent for your recent birthday.

Form: speeches

For **Paper 2**, you may be asked to write a speech.

Effective speech writing

Effective speeches can argue a point and persuade the listener.

Features of speeches:
- Personal examples to support viewpoint
- Short, direct statements to strengthen argument
- Challenges addressed and solutions offered
- Rhetorical devices to engage and persuade
- Facts and opinions as evidence to support opinion
- Counter-arguments to deal with opposing ideas
- Key points clearly signposted with adverbials

For more about rhetorical devices, see pages 27–28

Worked example

5 'Healthy eating is just as important as keeping fit.' Write a speech for a school assembly in which you explain your point of view on this statement. **(40 marks)**

This morning, I would like to talk to you about the importance of a healthy diet. The choices we make about the food we eat are crucial. As you know, fresh, nutritious meals and snacks are vital for strong teeth and bones, vital for healthy skin and hair, and vital for our energy levels and our mood. Without the proper nutrients, our physical and mental well being suffers. Furthermore, our academic performance is likely to be put at risk. What better reason, then, to rethink our approach to food? ...

- ✓ A clear, formal opening signals the purpose.
- ✓ Direct statement presents clear line of argument.
- ✓ Addresses the listener directly, presenting the ideas as points already agreed.
- ✓ Rhetorical devices (repetition, pattern of three, emotive language, rhetorical question) create a persuasive tone.
- ✓ Facts are used support personal opinions.
- ✓ Adverbials help to signpost the argument.

A full answer should include features such as counter-arguments and personal examples to strengthen the argument further.

Now try this

5 'It is important to approach revision in an organised way.' Write a speech for your year group assembly in which you explain your point of view on this statement. **(40 marks)**

Write the first **two** paragraphs of your speech. Try to use some of the features of effective speech writing discussed on this page.

Had a look ☐ Nearly there ☐ Nailed it! ☐

Putting it into practice

Paper 2, Section B: Writing tests your skills in **writing to present a viewpoint**. Look at the exam-style question below and read the extracts from two students' answers.

Worked example

5 'Teenagers do not contribute positively to society. All they do is cause trouble.'
Write an article for a national newspaper in which you explain your point of view on this statement. **(40 marks)**

Presenting a viewpoint

For questions like this you should:

- ✓ spend about **45 minutes** on your answer, including **planning and checking** time
- ✓ read the **question** carefully
- ✓ **annotate** the question to highlight the **purpose, audience and form**
- ✓ **plan** your answer.

Sample answer

Make the purpose of writing clear in your opening.

<u>Teenagers – humans or hoodlums?</u>

Some teenagers make an effort to contribute to society. 52% of teenagers at our local secondary school have received some form of reward or prize:

- Jane Smith won an art competition
- John Jones helped his neighbour in the garden
- Jake Johnson won first prize in a National Judo competition.

✓ Catchy headline, appropriate for the audience.

✗ There is no subheading to engage the reader or opening paragraph to introduce the subject and purpose.

✓ Use of statistics is appropriate for form and purpose.

✗ Although bullet points can be used in articles, detailed paragraphs would be a better way to establish the key points at the start of an article.

Improved sample answer

<u>Teenagers – dangerous or diligent?</u>

<u>Prejudices are pulled apart as our young people prove their positive impact on society</u>

A regular reader of this newspaper may well feel that all teenagers hang around on street corners, sipping from bottles of alcohol and spitting on passers-by. This image sells newspapers. But is it the whole story?

Positive stories do exist. I know of more teenagers who get it right than get it wrong. Some readers may choose to buy into the idea that all teenagers are trouble. However, take John Jones, for instance. Rather than idling on street corners, John has spent the last year giving up every weekend to help…

Notice how the subheading and developed opening paragraph help to make the purpose of writing clear in this answer.

✓ The rhetorical question engages the reader.

✓ The subheading helps in establishing the subject and purpose.

✓ The developed opening paragraph outlines the subject and gives a clear sense of form and audience.

✓ Developed paragraph details first key point.

✓ The adverbial 'however' neatly dismisses this well-placed counter-argument.

Now try this

In your own response to the **Paper 2** exam-style question above, write:

- a headline
- a subheading
- a short opening paragraph
- one developed paragraph about your first key point.

Try to use techniques that match the purpose. For example, rhetorical devices, evidence, counter-argument and adverbials.

Ideas and planning: creative

For **Paper 1, Section B: Writing** you will need to produce a **narrative** or a **description**. Planning is the best way to produce a well-structured and fully developed piece of writing.

Question options

You will be given **two question options** for the writing task in **Paper 1**. For example:

5 Your local newspaper is running a creative writing competition for teenagers.
Your entry will be judged by a panel of students your own age.

Either:

Write a description suggested by this picture:

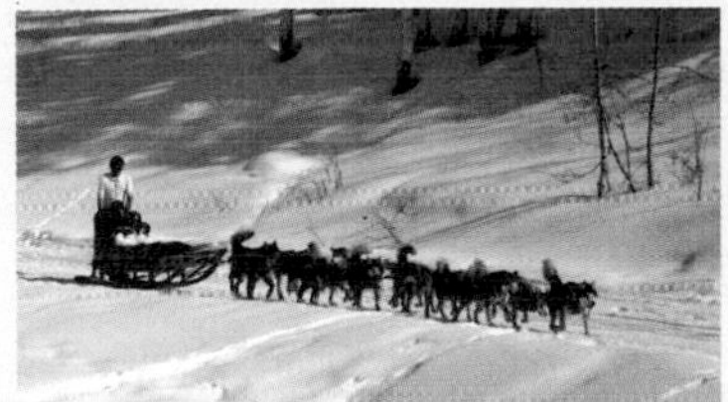

Or:

Describe an occasion when you helped someone.

(40 marks)

What you write about in the exam does not need to be based on a real, personal experience. You can make it up.

Getting it right

- Spend around **5 minutes planning**.
- **Choose the question** you are going to answer as quickly as you can. Which do you have the most initial ideas about?
- Think about which **narrative voice** to use. If you write about a real event that you have experienced yourself, use the first person.
- **Stay focused** on the question.
- Gather your **ideas** and organise them into **paragraphs**.
- Include ideas for **creative writing techniques**.

Turn to pages 54, 55, 80 and 84 for more about creative writing techniques

Now try this

Choose one of the **Paper 1** exam-style questions above. Gather and plan ideas for four or five paragraphs.

Ideas – picturing it

Picture the scene or event in your mind (or look at the image provided if you have chosen that option). Ask yourself:

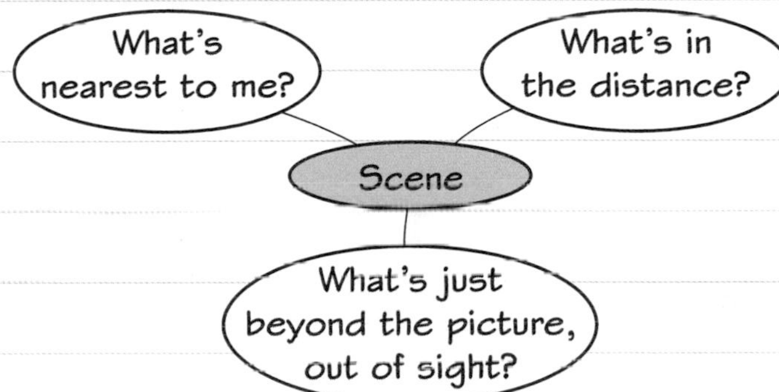
What's nearest to me?
What's in the distance?
Scene
What's just beyond the picture, out of sight?

Ideas – what's happening?

Think about the characters and action:

Characters
Who's there? – who are they?
What are they like?
How do they feel? – why?
What has brought these characters together?

Action
What is happening?
What are the characters doing?
What happened before?
What will happen next?

Turn to page 51 to refresh your memory about Paper 1, Section B: Writing

Planning

Plans can take various forms. A **spider diagram** keeps your ideas centred around the **main idea in the question**:

When I helped others – volunteering at homeless shelter, real experience, first person narrative

Recall conversation with old man, use dialogue to show character

Queues at mealtimes, use five senses to bring scene to life

Structure: creative

For **Paper 1: Section B: Writing** you will need to structure your **creative writing** effectively. The best way to achieve this is often to use some type of **narrative** structure.

Narrative structure

In the exam, you may write a short story. Short stories work best when they use a simple narrative structure like this:

1. **Exposition:** the beginning – Characters and setting established.
2. **Complication:** introduction of problem or conflict – Something begins to go wrong. This is the place for tension and excitement.
3. **Crisis:** the high point – The main event or danger faced by the character or characters.
4. **Resolution:** the ending – Conflicts are resolved, all loose ends are tied up and the story concludes on a happy or a sad note.

Many students spend too long on the exposition – setting the scene and describing the characters. Use this structure to plan and develop each part of your narrative.

Look at this student's structure plan for this exam-style question:

Worked example

5 Your school magazine wants to include examples of creative writing in the next edition.
Write a story about a change of plan. **(40 marks)**

Exposition: Woke up – excited – day out with boyfriend

Complication: Boyfriend phoned – finished with me. Mum tells me to stop sulking and help her at homeless shelter

Crisis: Meet person from my past at homeless shelter.

Resolution: Start working at homeless shelter

You could play with the narrative structure, starting at the crisis and using flashbacks to the exposition and complication – like this:
Crisis: Meet person from my past at homeless shelter.
Exposition: Remember waking up – excited – day out with boyfriend
Complication: Boyfriend phoned
Return to crisis: Mysterious stranger
Resolution...

✓ A clear narrative structure – each point can be expanded into more detailed paragraphs.

Now try this

Use this narrative structure to **plan** an answer to this **Paper 1** exam-style question:

5 Your school is running a creative writing competition.
Your entry will be judged by a panel of students your own age.
Write a short story about winning a prize. **(40 marks)**

Remember to plan where you will use appropriate creative writing techniques.

Beginnings and endings: creative

The **beginning** and **ending** of a piece of **creative writing** are very important. Both need to have an **impact** on the reader.

The beginning

This needs to:

- engage the reader immediately
- set the tone for the rest of your writing.
- You can do this with: a vivid description, dialogue, a mystery, or conflict or danger.

The beginning is sometimes called the 'exposition' or 'opening'.

With a vivid description

Glistening and gleaming in the evening haze, the sea spread out before us like a silver carpet. Waves lapped gently at the sides of the boat as we sailed silently along in the cool, salty breeze.

A good way to start if the setting plays a big role in your writing.

Opportunities to show your skills with imaginative writing techniques like figurative language.

With dialogue

"I'm scared. What do we do now?" Shadows flickered on Sarah's terrified face as she whispered her fears.

"Nothing," he hissed. "Keep quiet and just wait."

Gives the reader an immediate idea about one or more important characters.

With a mystery

I know I shouldn't have taken it. But I did. I'll be sorry for the rest of my miserable little life. It was only a tiny thing – but it caused so much trouble.

An engaging way to start if you want to use flashbacks.

Go to page 66 for more about narrative structure and flashbacks

The ending

The ending is the final impression the reader has of your writing. Follow these rules for a strong ending:

- **Plan** each stage of your writing in advance – you will be less likely to run out of time and rush at the end
- Spend time thinking about the **tone** of your ending – will it be happy, sad or funny?
- Craft your **final sentence** carefully – this is the last bit of your writing an examiner will read
- Avoid sudden mood changes – if the tone of your writing has been tense throughout, a happy ending is unlikely to work
- Avoid ending with a cliché like 'it was all a dream' – use your imagination!

With conflict or danger

I froze. Someone was in the house. I couldn't see them. But I knew they were there.

An effective way to create a sense of tension from the start.

Now try this

Look at this **Paper 1** exam-style question:

5 Your school is asking for examples of creative writing for its website.
Describe an occasion when you were home alone. **(40 marks)**

1 Write four possible openings using the techniques above. Use a different technique for each opening.

2 Choose one of your openings and write the final paragraph.

Had a look ☐ Nearly there ☐ Nailed it! ☐

Putting it into practice

Paper 1, Section B: Writing tests your **creative writing** skills. Planning before you write will help you produce a stronger answer. Look at the exam-style question below and the two students' plans.

Worked example

5 You are going to enter a creative writing competition run by a national newspaper. Your entry will be judged by people your own age. Write a short story about an unexpected visitor.

(40 marks)

Planning for creative writing

To plan for a question like this you should:

- spend about **5 minutes planning** your answer – the more detailed your plan is, the stronger your answer will be
- quickly decide **which question** to answer
- **plan** the narrative voice and creative writing techniques you will use
- create a **full and detailed plan**.

Sample plan

- Beginning – sitting in the lounge
- Complication – knock, then answer door, uses senses to show fear
- Opening the door …
- Crisis – stranger at door, use dialogue
- Ending – realise he is long-lost relative and invite him in

✓ Clear use of narrative structure.

✗ Details too brief in places and lack notes on creative writing techniques.

✗ Ending happens too soon and feels sudden and an anti-climax.

Improved sample plan

An unexpected visitor

Crisis – start with mystery – fear when door is opened and nobody there; create mysterious atmosphere with short sentence.

↓

Exposition – flashback using description of setting before knock on door, use senses to show calm feelings.

↓

Complication – knock on door, use metaphor for feelings.

↓

Crisis – reveal who is at door, stranger who hands over a package and then leaves, package has 'do not open' written on front; use personification of package to create tension.

↓

Resolution – describe examining the package and then finding, on the back 'until the morning'…

✓ Detailed use of narrative structure, using flashback to engage the reader.

✓ Detailed plan with notes about techniques to be used at each stage of the narrative.

✓ Resolution is planned to fully engage reader.

It is up to you to structure your plan in the way that works best for you. Note how this student has thought about both the structure and the techniques they will use.

Now try this

Finish the 'improved' plan above by completing the 'resolution', including your ideas for **creative writing techniques**.

Then write the first **two paragraphs** of an answer using this plan. Use one or more of the techniques for beginnings and endings from page 67.

Ideas and planning: viewpoint 1

Planning is the best way to make sure you produce a well-structured piece of writing that **argues** and **persuades** effectively. It will help you to **structure** your **writing** for **Paper 2, Section B: Writing** in a logical way and will help you fill your writing with relevant, imaginative ideas and carefully crafted language.

Worked example

5 'Watching television is a waste of everybody's time.'
Write an article for your local newspaper in which you explain your point of view on this statement. **(40 marks)**

Plan: TV is stealing your life

Intro

100s of channels run all day and all night

Average person watches 4 hours a day – a quarter of their waking life!

TV is passive not active ②

Evidence: my sister – hours spent staring, doing nothing.

Overweight and silent, TV is killing her brain and body.

TV is addictive ③

Once you start, it's difficult to turn off.

Evidence: watch least worst programme, not choosing what to watch.

~~Advertising is annoying~~

~~10/15 mins of it every hour – they want m~~y money!

~~Families~~ don't talk anymore ①

Evidence: Mine eats dinner in silence in front of the telly.

Some say it's educational and entertaining ④

It can be both – but how often? More often it's neither – e.g. Big Brother.

Conclusion

Most telly is a waste of time for everyone.

Choose what you want to watch – then turn it off.

Write your introduction, telling the reader what the situation is at the moment, and why that is a problem they need to think about.

Add some evidence to support each key point you make.

Plan key points by gathering together all the different ideas you can think of that support your viewpoint.

Don't be afraid to cross out some of your ideas.

Choose and sequence the most persuasive points. You will probably only need two or three key points.

Don't stop when you've thought of three ideas. Think of more, reject weaker ideas, then put the strong ideas in a logical order.

Add a counter-argument that gives an opposing viewpoint. Then say why you disagree.

Plan a conclusion – your final point to hammer home your argument.

Now try this

The plan above gives the view that television **is** a waste of time. Write a new plan in response to the exam-style question, giving the view that television **is not** a waste of time.

Ideas and planning: viewpoint 2

Planning is the best way to make sure you produce a well-structured piece of writing that aims to **inform** and/or **explain**. It will help you to **structure** your **writing** for **Paper 2, Section B: Writing** in the most effective way for the purpose, audience and form.

Worked example

5 'The facilities available locally for teenagers are inadequate and it is important that they are improved.'
Write a report for your local council in which you explain your point of view on this statement.

(40 marks)

Plan

Intro

- Firstly…not enough facilities
- Need to improve them
- Stop teenagers causing problems in town – could include statistics of recent trouble

1 Key point – Existing facilities

- Facts - what is available now
- Poor condition – give example of astro-turf & use expert opinion

2 Key point – Improvements suggested

- Youth club – re-decorate, could ask teenagers to help?
- Repair astro-turf, get grant from sports company.
- Add computers to local library

3 Key point – new facilities

- Bowling alley, give an estimate of how much money this could bring in
- Coffee shop – could be run by volunteers

Conclusion – finally…

- Explain benefit to other local people.

Plan an introduction that tells your reader what you are writing about and why it is important.

You will need three or four **key points**. These should be your main ideas.

Add ideas to each of your **key points**. You may decide to combine two key points in one paragraph, or divide one key point into two paragraphs.

Use temporal (time) adverbials to guide your reader through your points.

Use **appropriate techniques** to support the **audience and purpose**.

You might want to change the order of your paragraphs once you have written your plan.

Getting it right

Remember:

- you have about **45 minutes** to complete **the task, including planning and checking**
- your plan should include appropriate techniques for the form, audience and purpose.

Now try this

Look at this **Paper 2** exam-style question:

5 'Teenagers often find exams stressful. Schools need to do more to help students deal with exam stress.'
Write a report for your Headteacher in which you explain your point of view on this statement.

(40 marks)

Plan your answer. Aim to plan for three or four paragraphs, in addition to a short introduction and brief conclusion. Think carefully about the structure and the features and techniques you need to include to suit the audience and purpose.

Openings: viewpoint

Starting a piece of writing can be difficult. For **Paper 2**, know what you want to write, or you will be in danger of writing one or two boring paragraphs before you really get going.

An effective opening

Your first paragraph – and your first sentence in particular – needs to grab the reader's interest and attention. You could use.

- A bold and / or controversial statement:

> Experimenting on animals is a cruel necessity.

- A relevant quotation:

> 'What's in a name? That which we call a rose by any other name would smell as sweet.'
>
> (William Shakespeare, *Romeo and Juliet*, 2.2)

- A shocking or surprising fact or statistic:

> 99 per cent of the species that have ever lived on Planet Earth are now extinct.

- A rhetorical question:

> How many of us can honestly say that we care more about others than we do about ourselves?

- A short, relevant, **interesting** anecdote:

> When I was seven, my parents bought me a dog. This was when I first realised that …

Getting it right

Avoid telling the reader what you are going to write about:

In this essay I am going to argue that television is not a waste of time.

Just write it:

Television is informative, educational and interesting.

Introducing your topic

After your opening sentence, go on to introduce what you are writing about.

> … The average person spends a quarter of their waking life watching television. Are they making good use of their time? Or is television sucking the life out of them, killing them slowly with its mind-numbing mediocrity?

A surprising statistic shocks the reader and grabs their attention. Here, it invites the reader to compare how long they spend watching TV.

Two questions engage the reader, and present the two sides of the argument. The second question makes it clear which side the writer is on.

Now try this

Look at this **Paper 2** exam-style question:

> **5** 'There is more to school than passing exams.' Write an article for a national newspaper in which you explain your point of view on this statement. **(40 marks)**

1. Write **three** possible openings that would engage your reader's attention from the start.
2. Choose the most effective opening, then complete the introduction.

Had a look ☐ Nearly there ☐ Nailed it! ☐

Conclusions: viewpoint

For **Paper 2**, plan your conclusion before you start writing. Your final paragraph should leave your reader with a lasting impression.

Summing up

The final paragraph or conclusion to a text can be used to sum up your ideas – but avoid repeating them. Instead, aim to sum up and emphasise your central idea. You could use one or more of the following things.

Look back over your writing and sum it up neatly, leaving your reader with a clear message.

End on a vivid image: a picture that lingers in the reader's mind. A homeless person sits cold and alone in a shop doorway. As you pass by, you look into her eyes. She can't be older than 15.	**End on a warning:** what will happen if your ideas are not acted on? Within 50 years, the world will have changed beyond all recognition – and our children will blame us for what has happened.	**End on a happy note:** emphasise how great things will be if your ideas are acted on. Ours could be the generation that made the difference.
End on a thought-provoking question: leave the reader thinking. For how long can we ignore what is staring us in the face?	**Refer back to your introduction**, but don't repeat it. I still have that dog – and he's still incredibly badly behaved. But if I hadn't …	**End on a call to action:** make it clear what you want the reader to do. Don't just sit there. Get up, get out and make it happen.

Worked example

5 'Watching television is a waste of everybody's time.'
Write an article for your local newspaper in which you explain your point of view on this statement. **(40 marks)**

How many hours of television have you watched this week? What else could you have done with those hours? Television has turned us all into spectators – and while we're glued to the box, our lives are ticking away, wasted and unused. It's time to stop watching. It's time to start taking part.

Remember that questions engage the reader with the issue – how does it relate to their own life?

A warning

A final, powerful call to action

Now try this

Look at this **Paper 2** exam-style question:

5 'There is more to school than passing exams.'
Write an article for a national newspaper in which you explain your point of view on this statement. **(40 marks)**

Choose **one or more** of the above techniques to write a powerful conclusion.

Putting it into practice

Paper 2: Section B: Writing tests your skills in writing to present a **viewpoint**. Planning before you write will help you produce a stronger answer. Look at the exam-style question below and the two students' plans.

Worked example

5 'Video games are bad for teenagers' health and social lives.'
Write an article for your local newspaper in which you explain your point of view on this statement. **(40 marks)**

Planning to present a viewpoint

To plan for a question like this you should:

- spend **about 5 minutes planning** your answer – the more detailed your plan is, the stronger your answer will be
- **annotate** the question to highlight the **purpose, audience and form**
- **plan** the features and techniques you will use to support the **purpose, audience and form.**

Sample plan

Video games

- Good, educational, fun.
- Helps to build skills.
- Problems

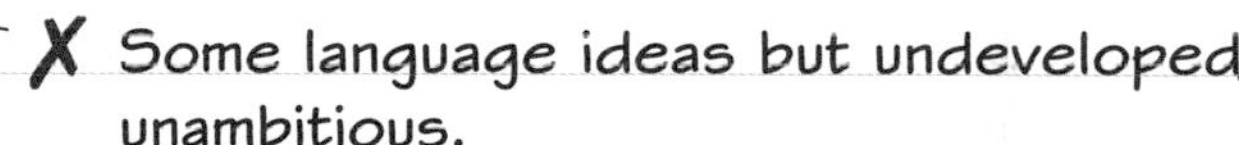

✗ Some language ideas but undeveloped/unambitious.

✗ Some ideas gathered, but more needed.

Make sure you provide a range of details for questions like this. In this plan, there is no detail added about the problems, the ideas are not sequenced, and there is no introduction or conclusion.

Improved sample plan

Gaming gambles with growing minds

1. Aggressive behaviour and poor concentration lead to problems at school; dismiss counter-argument about gaming skills like problem-solving

2. Physical problems – include obesity due to a less active lifestyle; could quote doctor here as evidence

3. Less opportunity to build relationships in the 'real' world; use rhetorical devices for emphasis

~~Sport is healthier~~

Intro: video games having a damaging effect on teenagers

Conclusion: important to take part in other activities, not just gaming.

✓ Ideas gathered and features of form (heading, counter-argument) included.

✓ Detail added.

✓ Less detailed, idea discarded.

Note that the answer is logically sequenced. Remember that effectively sequencing your ideas will improve your writing.

Now try this

Plan your own answer to the **Paper 2** exam-style question above and write an opening paragraph.

Remember to:

- gather, organise and sequence your ideas
- plan your introduction and conclusion.

Paragraphing

The best answers are organised into **paragraphs**. They help **structure** your writing, making it easier for the reader to follow your thinking and absorb your ideas. You will need to use paragraphs for your writing in **both papers**.

Paragraphs

Use paragraphs to divide your writing into clear points. Paragraphs help the reader follow your ideas and make the whole text more accessible.

one paragraph = one point

Planning can help you paragraph your writing. Make a clear plan, setting out all the points you want to make. Each time you start a new point, start a new paragraph.

Paragraphing for effect

In most cases you should start a new paragraph each time you start a new point. However, you can use shorter paragraphs for effect: to emphasise a point or create a dramatic pause.

A one-sentence paragraph can create a sense of tension and pace. Here, it leaves the reader in suspense about what actually happens to Ben. This will make them want to continue reading.

> Settling in front of the fire, Ben kicked off his shoes and stretched out his toes towards the warmth. Outside, rain battered the windows, through which he could just make out the autumn leaves as they danced around the garden and settled on the surface of the pond. Today was a good day to stay inside and relax.
>
> Later, Ben was to see that moment as his last real taste of freedom.
>
> The day had started much like any other. He had eaten his cereal, brushed his teeth, checked his bag and then left for school.

Use Point-Evidence-Explain to structure paragraphs in a piece of writing to argue or persuade.

- A short, clear **point**.
- **Evidence** to support the point.
- **Explains** how the point and evidence are relevant to the main idea.

> Britain's weather is changing. Barely a month goes by without it being declared the wettest, the driest, the hottest, the coldest, or the windiest month on record. Our weather is clearly becoming more extreme, and is likely to become even more so. How long can we ignore this before we act?

Structuring paragraphs: inform and explain

Start each paragraph with a **topic sentence** – a sentence that clearly introduces the reader to the content of this paragraph. Use the remainder of the paragraph to develop and add detail to the topic sentence.

- Topic sentence
- Detail / development

> Our school has made a huge effort to recycle its waste. Every classroom has a bin just for waste paper which is collected each week by student volunteers. In the canteen, we sort our rubbish into plastics, tin cans, and food waste. Even the staff room has three different bins so teachers can recycle!

Now try this

Write the next paragraph to either of the first two student answers above.

Linking ideas

Adverbials can be used to **guide** the reader through your ideas. They can work like **signposts**, showing the reader the direction your ideas are taking. Use adverbials to improve your writing for **both papers**.

Adding an idea

- Moreover …
- Furthermore …
- In addition …

This will not solve the situation. **Moreover**, it could make it worse.

Furthermore, this is likely to interrupt students' learning and add to their stress levels.

Explaining

- As a result
- Therefore
- Consequently

Science suggests that the teenage brain needs more sleep to help it grow and develop. **Consequently**, we spend longer in bed.

Teenagers' attitudes and actions are constantly challenged. It is **therefore** unsurprising that they sometimes challenge those who challenge them.

Illustrating

- For example
- For instance

For example, teenagers are frequently assumed to be responsible for graffiti and vandalism.

Emphasising

- In particular
- Especially
- Significantly

Significantly, these problems increased when the youth club was shut down.

Comparing and contrasting

Comparing

- Similarly
- Likewise
- In the same way

Contrasting

- However
- On the other hand
- On the contrary

It has been argued that an animal's life is not as valuable as that of a human being. **Similarly**, some have said that animals exist only because humans need them as a source of food. **However**, I would like to stress that…

Showing time

- Afterwards
- Previously
- Later
- At this moment
- After a while
- Meanwhile
- Before
- Then

Immediately **afterwards** he was to wonder what all the fuss had been about. **After a while** he was even able to see that he had dramatically over-reacted. But at the point when the door swung open, Ben had no thought in his head beyond…

Now try this

Read this student's writing. Add a range of adverbials to link the ideas together and guide the reader through them.

This morning, my sister proved that she is the most annoying person on earth. She finished all the milk so there was none left for me. She spent an hour in the bathroom. She borrowed my headphones without asking and wouldn't give them back. She can be thoughtful. She made me a delicious lasagne the other day. She always remembers my birthday and buys me great presents.

Had a look ☐ Nearly there ☐ Nailed it! ☐

Putting it into practice

For **both papers**, you need to structure your writing in a way that makes it easy for the reader to follow. Using paragraphs and adverbials will help you to do this. Look at the **Paper 2** exam-style question below and read the extracts from two students' answers.

Worked example

5 'Learning to use computers would offer many benefits to the elderly.'
Write an article for your local newspaper in which you explain your point of view on this statement. **(40 marks)**

Paragraphing and adverbials

For each writing question you should:

- ✓ write in paragraphs
- ✓ plan one point per paragraph
- ✓ use adverbials to guide your reader through the text.

Sample answer extract

One of the most popular things you can do on the internet is social networking. You can go on websites like Facebook and keep in touch with all your friends. You can also use online encyclopedias to find out about anything you want to know. You can also use the internet to save your photos and share them with your friends and relatives on websites like Facebook.

✓ A clear point supported with evidence.

✗ This evidence should be supported with a persuasive explanation.

✗ This point should have been sequenced to develop the first point, using the adverbial to guide the reader.

Remember that a new point should mean a new paragraph. Remember also to support your points with evidence or an explanation. This point contains neither.

Improved sample answer

The internet is a modern miracle: a world of information at your fingertips, waiting to be discovered. Thanks to clever websites called 'search engines', all you have to do is type in a few words and up will pop an enormous choice of websites. It's so simple, even people with limited experience of computers can surf the internet with ease.

There are many things older people can do on computers, making every day life easier for them. For example, you can email friends and relations around the world, sharing your news and views in just a few clicks. It's much quicker than writing a letter – and saves money on stamps.

✓ Paragraph clearly organised using:

- point
- evidence
- explanation.

Note here the accurate paragraphing, with links back to the previous paragraph. Note also an adverbial phrase (For example) to introduce evidence.

Now try this

Plan and write the next **two** paragraphs of the 'improved sample answer' above. You could develop some of ideas already mentioned.

Getting it right

Remember:

- write in paragraphs
- use P-E-E. to structure your paragraphs
- use adverbials to link your paragraphs.

Formality and standard English 1

It is vital that the **language** you use is appropriate for the **purpose** and **audience** of your writing. This is especially important for **Paper 2, Section B: Writing**.

colloquial language: informal language that is not rude and is often used in speech, but would not be used in formal situations

register: the formality of the language appropriate to a particular purpose or in a particular social setting

slang: language at its most informal, which can be described as non-standard and ungrammatical; often used within particular social groups and more common in speech than writing

standard English: the form of English considered to be the usual, correct form of the language

Formal and informal language

For most purposes and audiences, you will need to use formal language. This means writing in standard English.

In some cases, it may be appropriate to use carefully chosen colloquial or informal language, for example if your audience is a friend or is younger than you. However, you should still avoid slang. Even less formal language needs to be clearly understood, and you should still aim to show off a wide range of vocabulary choices and sentence structures.

Another word for the level of formality of the language you use is **register**.

He's **minted**. — Slang

He's **made of money**. — Colloquial, informal language

He's **wealthy**. — Standard English

Choosing the appropriate register

Always choose the register that is most suitable for your purpose and audience.

This student is writing to a close friend to describe a recent holiday:

I write to you with regard to my recent holiday to Paris. Highlighted below is a selection of the moments about which I feel compelled to inform you.

The register is far too formal for the purpose and audience. A friend would expect an entertaining letter, with some informal language.

This student is writing to her local MP:

We need money now to sort out the park as it's hopeless – there's nothing to do and you don't care about the kids and just care about yourself and your posh mates.

The language is extremely informal, which is inappropriate for the audience – an MP. The tone is aggressive, too, and unlikely to support the purpose – to persuade.

Now try this

The text below aims to persuade Year 11 students that revision is key to a successful career. It is very informal and uses some slang. Rewrite the text, using a more appropriate register.

You reckon the dough's just gonna roll in, yeah? You're gonna get minted without lifting a finger? Dream on! If u want success, then it's all about the hard slog. Get stuck into that revision now! It ain't gonna happen overnight.

Take care to avoid texting language.

Had a look ☐ Nearly there ☐ Nailed it! ☐

Formality and standard English 2

Before you start to write, particularly for **Paper 2, Section B: Writing**, think carefully about the **purpose** and **audience** of your writing. Then choose the appropriate **register**.

Ways to make your writing more formal

You can make your writing more formal in a variety of ways. For example:

	Less formal		More formal
✓ Use more sophisticated or technical vocabulary	The **ambulance man** helped...	→	The **paramedic** assisted...
✓ Replace unnecessary colloquial expressions	I was **sort of thinking of maybe going to the footie.**	→	I was **considering attending the football match.**
✓ Use abstract nouns	It was a **stupid decision** that cost him his job.	→	It was **stupidity** that cost him his job.
✓ Use adverbials to link your ideas clearly	The local facilities are in poor repair **so** it is time...	→	The local facilities are in poor repair; **consequently**, it is time...
✓ Use the passive voice instead of the active voice.	**We told** the police.		The police **were informed**.

Worked example

5 'Online shopping only leads to dissatisfied customers who struggle to return faulty items.'
Write an article for a national newspaper in which you explain your point of view on this statement. **(40 marks)**

The number of <u>consumers</u> forced to lodge complaints about products <u>purchased</u> online is rising rapidly. <u>Furthermore</u>, it is increasingly likely that these <u>grievances</u> must be pursued <u>over a number of months</u>, until the offending outlets are finally persuaded to replace the faulty item or issue a refund.

✓ Use of sophisticated, formal language.

✓ More complex adverbials are used to guide the reader.

✓ Language is carefully chosen to avoid colloquial expressions; here, a less formal, and therefore less appropriate, choice might have been 'for ages'.

Now try this

Your friend has asked you to look over his letter of application for a work experience position at a local newspaper. An extract from the letter is below. Focus on the language he has used. What suggestions would you give?

> I love newspapers, especially the *Herald* – it's gr8. Is there ny chance you could give me some work experience? My English teacher says I have a good gut about how newspaper articles work and I am sure I will impress you with my enthusiastic attitude.

Vocabulary for effect: synonyms

Synonyms are words with similar meanings. Use them in your writing for **both papers** to avoid repetition and to add variety.

Using synonyms

Using synonyms can make your writing more varied and interesting. Having a range of synonyms for key words and ideas in mind as you write will mean that:

- you don't repeat the same key word throughout your writing
- you can pick the most precise word – the one that really says what you want it to say.

Be your own thesaurus

You know hundreds – perhaps thousands – of words that you rarely use. So you don't need a thesaurus to come up with ambitious, effective vocabulary chosen for its impact. You just need to think through your mental thesaurus. Beware though! Don't use a word if you are not absolutely sure of its precise meaning.

Examples of synonyms

Comments on evidence often involve the phrase This suggests … Replace it with:

- This gives the impression that …
- It seems clear that …
- This implies …
- In other words …

Arguments are often about ideas. To avoid repeating the word idea, you could use:

- notion
- point
- concept
- opinion
- viewpoint

Worked example

5 'Celebrities have too much influence on our lives.'
Write an article for your school or college magazine in which you argue for or against this statement. **(40 marks)**

The idea of celebrities as perfect role models is not the only misguided idea connected with the world of the celebrity. Some people have the idea that celebrities should be consulted on everything from international politics to haircare.

Repetition can add pace and rhythm to your writing – but there are too many words being repeated too often here, weakening an otherwise strong paragraph.

Getting it right

Using the same word more than once can undo all the hard work you put into an answer, making your ideas seem repetitive and uninteresting.

Now try this

Rewrite the student's answer from the Worked example, replacing the words 'celebrities', 'celebrity' and 'idea' with different synonyms.

Before you start, make a list of all the synonyms you can think of for the word 'celebrity'. You can use a thesaurus if you get stuck.

Had a look ☐ Nearly there ☐ Nailed it! ☐

Vocabulary for effect: creative

Choosing the most effective vocabulary can have a significant impact on your writing, especially when you are writing to **describe** in **Paper 1**.

Don't overdo it

When writing to describe, it is important that you do just that. However, be careful not to overdo it.

Avoid piling on the adjectives and adverbs:

✗ The sun's glorious golden rays burst through my gleaming windows, sending shimmering sparkling beams of incandescence dancing around my walls.

Describe what matters – not what doesn't

Don't describe everything. Focus on what matters. For example, if you want to describe a phone call shattering an awkward silence, focus on the relevant detail:

✗ The insistent ringtone of the phone suddenly filled the room so I hurried to the low, wooden table on which it sat and picked up the slim black handset, pressing it to my ear.

✓ The jangling phone made me jump. I answered it.

The best words

The best description often uses fewer, well-chosen words that **show** the reader, rather than **tell** them. Carefully chosen verbs can be especially effective:

✗ He walked across the room with a spring in his step.

✓ He bounced across the room.

✗ He flung open the door and walked quickly into the room.

✓ He flew into the room.

However, sometimes showing the reader takes more words than telling them. Here are a couple of rules.

Don't name your feelings:

✗ I felt really really terrified.

✓ I clenched my clammy palms into fists and tried to stop my legs shaking.

Do describe the effect they have on you:

✗ It hurt a lot.

✓ Pain shot through me like a thunderbolt.

Describing people

Choose just one or two details that will give the reader an impression of a person. For example, three of the details opposite could be used to show the reader that this person is concerned about their appearance. The others tell you very little.

✗ Brown hair
✗ Brown eyes
✗ Glasses
✗ Dark trousers
✓ Wearing a tie
✓ Highly polished shoes
✓ Finger with wedding ring mark

Now try this

Write the opening paragraph of your response to this **Paper 1** exam-style question.

5 You are going to enter a creative writing competition run by your local newspaper.
Your entry will be judged by students your own age.
Describe an occasion when you faced a fear.

(40 marks)

Remember:
- your task is to describe, not to tell a story, so focus on describing the situation, your thoughts and feelings
- choose only relevant details to describe
- choose the best words that show the reader how you felt.

Vocabulary for effect: viewpoint

When writing to **present a viewpoint** in **Paper 2**, you need to be able to use a wide vocabulary of **emotive words** and **positive and negative language**.

Vocabulary for impact

Using emotive language can add impact to an argument. For example, you may think that global warming is a problem. To shock your reader into action, you want to emphasise the problem by choosing a more emotive word:

If we ignore global warming now, we will soon be facing a ~~problem~~

catastrophe | disaster | calamity

Add even more power to your sentence by intensifying the emotive word:

horrific | alarming | terrifying

we will soon be facing a terrifying catastrophe.

Positive and negative

If you frame your ideas in **positive** or **negative** language you can control your reader's reaction to them. For example,

If you **support** fox hunting, it could be described as 'a humane method of pest control'.

If you **oppose** fox hunting, it could be described as 'a cruel and barbaric sport'.

If you are arguing in **support** of typical teenage behaviour, you could point out that: 'Sleep is an essential ingredient for the teenage brain's development.'

Taking the **opposing point of view** you might write: 'Idle teenagers lounge in bed for hours, paralysed by their crippling laziness.'

Connotations

You can guide your reader's reaction by thinking about the connotations of your vocabulary choice. Look at these words. Each one has a similar meaning but carries different associations.

Six hours of intensive revision can make you ...

- exhausted. — extreme, intense
- drained. — implies weak, empty
- sleepy. — sounds childish, mocking

Fox hunting is ...

- brutal. — emphasises violence
- barbaric. — suggests uncivilised
- heartless. — emphasises lack of feeling or empathy

Now try this

Write the opening paragraph of your response to this **Paper 2** exam-style question.

> **5** 'School is cruel.'
> Write an article for your local newspaper in which you explain your point of view on this statement. **(40 marks)**

Remember to choose vocabulary for its impact and for its connotations.

Language for different effects 1

Language techniques can add **power** and **impact** when you write to present a **viewpoint** in **Paper 2** and in your **creative** writing for **Paper 1**.

Rhetorical questions

Use these in argument or persuasive writing to lead the reader to the answer you want.

There is really only one way to answer this question:

> Would you stand by and do nothing if you saw a human being treated like this?

You can also use them in descriptive writing to engage the reader in a situation:

> What was going on?

> Could I trust him again?

Contrast

Place two opposing ideas or situations in direct contrast to emphasise the difference.

> You can work hard in a job you hate for the rest of your life …

> or you can work hard on your GCSEs for a couple of years and get the job you want.

You can also use contrast in descriptive writing to exaggerate a detail: 'Among all the smiling, happy faces there was just one exception: my father's sour-faced, snarling scowl.'

Repetition

Repeating a word or phrase can emphasise a key point or idea in an argument:

> Chasing a helpless animal across fields is cruel. Setting dogs on a helpless animal is cruel. Watching as the dogs butcher the helpless animal is cruel.

It can also add emphasis to an idea in descriptive writing:

> There is no point in discussing it, there is no point in arguing about it, there is no point in shouting about it. Once my father has made up his mind, it is made up.

Lists

Use a list to suggest a range of ideas in your persuasive writing:

> It's quick, simple, easy and cheap.

> The improvement would be huge: students would learn more, learn faster, be more motivated, enjoy school more and achieve better results.

Use it to suggest range or variety in your descriptive writing:

> Scattered across the carpet were balloons, paper hats, streamers and torn shreds of wrapping paper.

Now try this

Choose **one** of these exam-style questions. Write **four** short extracts in response to your chosen question. Use **one** of the language techniques above in each extract.

Paper 1:

5 Your school is asking for examples of creative writing for its website.
Describe an occasion when you visited a favourite place. **(40 marks)**

Paper 2:

5 'It is important to take exercise and lead a healthy life.'
Write an article for your school newspaper in which you explain your point of view on this statement. **(40 marks)**

Language for different effects 2

Language techniques can add **power** and **impact** when you write to present a **viewpoint** in **Paper 2** and in your **creative** writing for **Paper 1**.

Direct address

Talking directly to the reader is persuasive. Using the **second person 'you'** can suggest that your ideas are relevant to their lives. For example:

'**you** can get involved in lots of different ways'

involves the reader and is much more persuasive than:

'There are many ways to get involved.'

Using the **first person plural 'we'** can create a relationship between you, the writer, and the reader. It suggests that we are all in the same situation, facing the same problems:

'If **we** do nothing, then nothing will change. It is up to us to act and act now.'

Pattern of three

Putting words or phrases in linked groups of three adds rhythm and emphasis to your ideas in all kinds of writing:

It doesn't matter if you're a beginner, an improver or an expert. It's fun for everyone!

It will benefit the students, the teachers and the community as a whole.

I approached the front door. My hands were cold, clammy and shaking.

Alliteration

Alliteration can add rhythm and emphasis to your writing. Remember: the alliterative words do not have to be *next* to each other – just *near* each other.

It was a truly terrifying experience.

Combined with other language techniques, alliteration can be particularly engaging and powerful: 'It's fun, fast and furious.'

Hyperbole

Exaggeration can add humour to an argument or a description:

The house looked like a herd of elephants had run through it, detonating hand grenades as they went.

It can also emphasise a key point:

Teachers want their students to sit completely still and in total silence for six hours a day.

Now try this

Choose **one** of these exam-style questions. Write **four** short extracts in response to your chosen question, using **one** of the language techniques above in each extract.

Paper 1:

5 Your school is asking for contributions for an anthology of creative writing.
Describe an occasion when you felt under pressure. **(40 marks)**

Paper 2:

5 'Mobile phones are killing young people's ability to communicate.'
Write a letter to your local newspaper in which you argue for or against this statement. **(40 marks)**

Had a look ☐ Nearly there ☐ Nailed it! ☐

Language for different effects 3

You can use **figurative language** to create powerful images in your readers' minds. You should certainly use figurative language in your **creative writing** for **Paper 1**. If you use it carefully (and not too often!), figurative language can also show imagination and originality when you write to present a **viewpoint** in **Paper 2**.

Similes

A simile is a comparison, usually using **as** or **like**, suggesting a resemblance between one thing and another. It can be used:

- **to inform**

When you get it right, skateboarding can be as exhilarating as a skydive from 30,000 feet.

- **to persuade**

Smoking cigarettes is like a game of Russian roulette – and the chances are, you'll end up losing.

Metaphor

A metaphor is a direct comparison suggesting a resemblance between one thing and another. It can be used when writing:

- **to argue**

At night, when there is nothing else to do, the youth club is a bright light in the darkness, drawing all the young people of the town through its doors.

- **to describe**

She stared and stared, her eyes burning holes in my face.

Personification

Personification is the technique of describing something non-human as if it were human. It can be used when writing:

- **to describe**

Sunlight danced on the water as we headed out to sea.

- **to persuade**

Smoking is highly addictive and, once the habit has got its hands around your throat, it will not let go.

Getting it right

Remember these dos and don'ts.

- **Don't** try to force one simile, one metaphor and one personification into each answer.
- **Do** look for opportunities where figurative language will add impact to your ideas.
- **Do** avoid clichés – try to be original and try to avoid using comparisons like 'cool as a cucumber' or 'white as a sheet', which your reader will have read a hundred times before.

Now try this

Choose **one** of these exam-style questions. Write **three** short extracts in response to your chosen question. Use **one** of the language techniques above in each extract.

Paper 1:

5 Your local council wants to display examples of creative writing as part of the annual arts festival. Describe an occasion when you met a hero. **(40 marks)**

Paper 2:

5 'Young people grow up too fast. We should let children be children for as long as possible.' Write an article for a broadsheet newspaper in which you explain your point of view on this statement. **(40 marks)**

Putting it into practice

For **Paper 1**, you will need to show you can use language effectively in **creative writing**. Look at the exam-style question below and read the extracts from two students' answers.

Worked example

5 You are going to enter a creative writing competition.
Your entry will be judged by students your age.
Describe an occasion when you made a mistake.
(40 marks)

Language choice

In each of your writing tasks you should:

- ✓ choose language appropriate to your audience
- ✓ make ambitious and effective vocabulary choices to engage your reader
- ✓ use a range of language techniques.

Sample answer extract

The worst mistake I ever made was jumping out of a tree. I was down the park with my friends and they dared me to climb this really tall tree. I was about eight. So I climbed up the tree. I got about a metre up and it felt like I was nearly at the sky. I looked down and realised I hadn't got very far and they were all laughing and shouting and encouraging me to go higher. So I carried on climbing. I went up another metre or so. By now I was really scared.

✗ Language choice too informal.

✗ Limited description, and unambitious vocabulary choice.

✓ Effective use of figurative language.

Note that although there is some limited (but effective) language choice here, there are also missed opportunities to use really effective language (as you can see in the final sentence).

Improved sample answer

My aunt had come to stay. She was a stern, grey-faced woman with eyes that could turn you to stone. When she entered a room, an arctic cold crept through the air, freezing you instantly into silence. The only thing that would make my aunt crack her face and bring out a smile was cake. She loved it. Cream cake, chocolate cake, fruit cake, any cake would bring a rosy glow to her cheeks and her long, sharpened teeth out from between her grey lips. And that was where the trouble started.

✓ Engaging vocabulary choice.

✓ Effective use of language devices:

- metaphor
- personification
- list.

Notice how this language choice shows humour as well as being effective.

Now try this

Write the **first two** paragraphs of your own answer to the **Paper 1** exam-style question above.

Remember to choose and use:

- language appropriate to your audience
- language for effect
- a range of ambitious vocabulary and language features.

Putting it into practice

For **Paper 2,** you will need to show you can use language effectively when you write to **present a viewpoint**. Look at the exam-style question below and read the extracts from two students' answers.

Worked example

5 'Families with young children should not be allowed to own dogs.'
Write an article for a broadsheet newspaper in which you explain your point of view on this statement. **(40 marks)**

Using language to present a viewpoint

For questions like this you should:

- choose **language** that is ambitious and appropriate for the **purpose and audience**
- choose **language techniques** with care and for **impact**
- **avoid** using **too many** techniques – it is more important that your writing is well structured and appropriate for the purpose and audience.

Sample answer extract

Why do parents think that letting their kids have a dog is a good idea?

This week we heard about another kid being bitten in his own home by the family pet. The baby did not die, but will be scarred for life. And what will be the effect of being bitten by an animal he loved?

✓ Rhetorical questions set out key point at start and keep the reader engaged.

✗ Language too informal for purpose, audience and form.

✓ Use of evidence to support point.

✗ Unimaginative vocabulary means the writing is less persuasive.

Improved sample answer

Why do parents feel children's lives will be enhanced by dog ownership? For all of the upsides – and I appreciate that dogs can become a real part of the family – attacks by man's best friend have increased by 40% in the last year alone.

Yet again this week, we heard about another toddler being savaged in his own home by the family pet. Luckily, the baby did not die, but he will carry the scars for the rest of his life. And what about the consequences of being brutally mauled by a beloved and trusted member of the family?

✓ Rhetorical question, with the appropriately formal language 'children', indicates the article will be serious and factual.

✓ Statistics supply evidence in the opening paragraph to create trustworthy tone.

✓ A wide range of (correctly spelt) ambitious vocabulary is used for emotive effect.

Turn to pages 96–98 for more about spelling

This answer uses language effectively. Emotive words and phrases are used to shock the reader, and statistics are used to support the points made. Remember that statistics don't need to be real, but they do need to be believable.

Now try this

Complete the 'improved student answer' above. Remember to include a counter-argument and use adverbials to link your key points and paragraphs.

See pages 56 and 61 for reminders about presenting a viewpoint and writing articles

Sentence variety 1

Using a range of **different sentence types** when you write to present a **viewpoint** and in your **creative writing** can help you convey your ideas clearly and effectively and keep your readers engaged.

Engaging the reader

Writing for young children uses a limited range of sentence types:

> Penny went out of the house.
> It was raining.
> Soon she was soaked.
> Penny turned around and went home again.

Effective writing for adults uses a variety of sentence types to hold the reader's interest.

Sentence types

These are the basic types of sentence:

- Single-clause
- Multi-clause
- Minor

To remind yourself which is which, look back at page 31. You will probably want to use all these types in your writing.

Multi-clause sentences

Multi-clause sentences can help you to keep your readers engaged with your ideas. These are the main types.

Sentences using a subordinate clause

- This is additional information which is added to the main clause using conjunctions such as: because, although, if, since.
- The subordinate clause is dependent on the main clause because it doesn't make sense without it.

Subordinate clause — Main clause

> Before I went out, I locked all the doors.

You can often swap the main and subordinate clauses without changing the meaning of the sentence.

Sentences using a coordinate clause

If neither clause is dependent on the other, then the clauses are coordinate. Coordinate clauses use conjunctions such as and, but, or.

Main clause — These clauses are an equal pair.

> I checked that the windows were shut and I locked the front door.

Sentences using a relative clause

This is where additional information is introduced using a **relative pronoun**, such as: that, where, which, whose, who, when.

Main clause — Relative clause, separated from the main clause with commas

> The neighbour, who I've never liked, waved as I walked down the front path.

Now try this

Write the opening paragraph of a response to this **Paper 1** exam-style question:

> **5** You are going to enter a national creative writing competition.
> Your entry will be judged by students your own age.
> Write a short story about moving house. **(40 marks)**

Aim to use at least **one** of each sentence type:

- A single-clause sentence
- A multi-clause sentence with
  - a subordinate clause
  - a coordinate clause
  - a relative clause
- A minor sentence

Had a look ☐ Nearly there ☐ Nailed it! ☐

Sentence variety 2

Thinking about the **first word** of your sentences can help you **add interest** to your **writing** for **both papers**.

First words

Developing writers often start their sentences in similar ways. Try to start your sentences in different ways to engage your reader. You can start with any of these.

Type of word	Examples
A pronoun I, you, he, she, it, we, they, my, your	I turned and started.
An article a, an, the	The glass had disappeared.
A preposition above, behind, between, near, with, etc.	Above me, I heard footsteps.
An -ing word (or present participle) running, hurrying, crawling, smiling, etc.	Edging silently to the door, I went to the stairs and listened.
An adjective slow, quiet, huge, violent, etc.	Sharp, prickling pains crept from my fingertips to my hair.
An adverb alarmingly, painfully, happily, etc.	Gingerly, I put my foot on the first stair.
A conjunction (subordinate clause + main clause) if, although, because, when, while, etc.	Although I knew I was in an empty house, I could not help thinking that I was not alone.

Now try this

Write the first **ten** sentences for this **Paper 1** exam-style question:

> **5** Your school is creating a wall display of creative writing for parents' evening. Describe your most memorable moment at school. **(40 marks)**

Have a go at:
- using all seven different types of sentence opener in your writing
- using a variety of sentence types.

Sentences for different effects

Structuring your sentences in different ways can achieve different effects. For example, it can help you to emphasise an argument when you write to **present a viewpoint**, or to achieve a particular mood in your **creative writing**.

Longer sentences

Use longer, **multi-clause sentences** to deliver more information sharply and concisely. You can add information using one or more subordinate clauses, as the example opposite shows.

Beware: if you overload a sentence with too much information, spread over a number of subordinate clauses, you could lose your reader's attention.

Main clause — Relative clause

The house, which I had never visited before, seemed strangely familiar.

Notice how the clauses have been separated with commas.

The long and the short

Short, punchy, single-clause sentences can be particularly effective: they add impact to an argument, and surprise or tension to a description. Look at the contrast opposite.

Short, single-clause sentences are particularly effective when they follow a longer, multi-clause, sentence.

Long sentence to contrast with a short sentence to surprise.

Some people believe in leaping out of bed as the sun is rising and settling down to an hour's revision before breakfast, then a couple of hours' more revision before a short jog to revive the brain and another couple of hours' revision before lunchtime. I do not.

In order of importance

You can structure your sentences for emphasis. Important information is usually placed at the end of a sentence.

Arrange your sentences so that the point you want to emphasise comes at the end.

- This sentence gives more emphasis to the revision than the exams because it comes at the end of the sentence:

The final insult is that the dreaded exams come after all that revision.

- This sentence emphasises the dreaded exams, giving the sentence more impact:

The final insult is that after all that revision come the dreaded exams.

Now try this

Write **one** or **two** paragraphs in response to the **Paper 2** exam-style opposite.

Aim to include:

- a long sentence followed by a short sentence
- a sentence structured to leave the important information until the end.

5 'Sport and life are quite similar. In both of them, the only thing that matters is winning.'
Write a speech for a Year 11 assembly in which you argue for or against this statement.
(40 marks)

Putting it into practice

For **both papers** you will need to show you can vary your sentences for effect. Look at the **Paper 2** exam-style question below and read the extracts from two students' answers.

Worked example

5 'It is important to follow fashion and look good.' Write an article for a broadsheet newspaper in which you explain your point of view on this statement. **(40 marks)**

Sentence variety

In each of the writing tasks you should:

- ✓ use a range of sentence structures
- ✓ start your sentences in different ways
- ✓ structure your sentences for effect.

Sample answer extract

Fashion is important because people judge you on how you look, even though you shouldn't it's difficult not to. Fashion can also be fun because shopping and choosing clothes and seeing what your friends are wearing is really enjoyable. Fashion is also something to talk about and do with your friends because if all your friends are in fashion and like the same fashion then you can swap clothes and tell them how they look.

Notice that:

- each sentence starts in the same way
- each sentence follows the same structure
- sentences are all long, with multiple clauses.

To improve your answer you should add variety to engage the reader.

✗ Vocabulary is frequently repeated.

✗ A limited range of adverbials and conjunctions creates repetitive vocabulary and sentence structure.

Improved sample answer

We all judge a book by its cover. We don't mean to but we do. But should we?

Even if we don't want to judge others, we expect others to judge us. We primp, preen and polish ourselves for hours, preparing ourselves to be seen by the world. How disappointing would it be if, after all that effort, no one bothered to look and make the right judgement?

The truth is that, no matter how much we might not want appearances to matter, they do. They matter very much.

Notice how this answer starts with:

- two short sentences to create an emphatic opening
- a rhetorical question to engage the reader
- a neatly structured sentence.

The improvement is reflected in the grade.

✓ A second rhetorical question further engages the reader.

✓ Long sentence, followed by powerful short sentence further emphasised with repetition.

Now try this

Write the **first two** paragraphs of your own answer to the **Paper 2** exam-style question above.

Ending a sentence

In **both papers** your writing will be marked for the quality of your **punctuation**. Make sure you start each sentence with a **capital letter**. End each sentence with a **full stop, an exclamation mark or a question mark.**

Check your full stops

Most students know that a sentence should start with a capital letter and end with a full stop. However, mistakes are often made. The most common error is using a comma to join two sentences instead of a full stop to separate them. This is called a **comma splice.**

Avoiding the comma splice

When you want to tell the reader two pieces of information you can do two things.

✓ Separate them with a full stop:

> The countryside is green and peaceful. It can sometimes be too quiet.

✓ Join them with a conjunction:

> The countryside is green and peaceful **but** it can sometimes be too quiet.

✗ You cannot join them with a comma:

> The countryside is green and peaceful, it can sometimes be too quiet.

Question marks

Always check you have actually put a question mark at the end of a question – especially if it is a rhetorical question.

Exclamation marks

Be **very** careful in your use of exclamation marks. Follow these golden rules:

- Only use an exclamation mark for a real exclamation, e.g. 'Thank goodness!' he cried.
- Use them very sparingly. Don't scatter them randomly throughout your writing.
- Never use two or more exclamation marks in a row.

Now try this

Rewrite this student's answer, removing all the comma splices. Try to do this in three different ways by:

- adding conjunctions
- restructuring some of the sentences
- replacing the comma splices with full stops.

> I was born in the countryside, I grew up surrounded by the sounds and smells of the natural world, when I was ten we moved to the city; it was a confusing, fast-paced, deafening environment that I found hard to love. It was such a big change, it came as quite a shock to my system, worst of all I had to leave all my friends behind and try to make new ones in this strange, unfamiliar place. I was lonely, convinced I would never feel at home, before a year had passed I had the best friend anyone could wish for.

Remember that you do not use a comma to join two pieces of information in a sentence. Use a full stop to separate them, or a conjunction to join them.

Had a look ☐ Nearly there ☐ Nailed it! ☐

Commas

It is very important that you feel confident using **commas**, as you will need to use them to create **effective multi-clause sentences** and **lists**.

Turn to pages 87–88 for a reminder about sentence types

Commas and subordinate clauses

In a multi-clause sentence, the main clause and the subordinate clause can usually be swapped around without changing the meaning of the sentence:

I meet new people (main clause) wherever I go. (subordinate clause)

If you begin a multi-clause sentence with the main clause, there is no need for a comma to separate the clauses.

Wherever I go, (subordinate clause) I meet new people. (main clause)

If you begin a multi-clause sentence with the subordinate clause, use a comma to separate it from the main clause.

Commas and relative clauses

You can add a relative clause to a sentence, giving additional information linked with one of these relative pronouns:

- that
- who
- whose
- which
- where
- when

You should always separate the relative clause from the main clause with commas.

Main clause / Relative clause

The house, which I had never visited before, seemed strangely familiar.

Notice how the clauses have been separated with commas.

Commas in a list

If you are writing a list, add a comma after each word or phrase – apart from the words or phrases which are linked using and.

- Use commas in lists of adjectives:

He was tall, smartly dressed and elegant.

Comma here to separate two items in a list.

No comma here because they are linked with and.

- Use commas in lists of phrases:

There was mud on the floor, mud on the walls, mud on the windows and mud on the ceiling.

Now try this

Look at this **Paper 2** exam-style question:

5 'Your school days are the happiest days of your life.'
Write an article for your local newspaper in which you explain your point of view on this statement. **(40 marks)**

Write **three** to **five** sentences, using commas correctly to separate:

- items in a list
- a main and subordinate clause
- a main and relative clause

End your sentences correctly. Avoid using a **comma splice**.

Had a look ☐ Nearly there ☐ Nailed it! ☐

Apostrophes and speech punctuation

Missing or incorrect **apostrophes** and **speech punctuation** are common errors. You may need to use dialogue in **both papers**, so make sure you know how to avoid mistakes.

Apostrophes in contractions

When two words are shortened or abbreviated, some letters are missed out or omitted. You should use an apostrophe to show where these letters are missing:

cannot → **can't**
do not → **don't**
I will → **I'll**
let us → **let's**

Abbreviations such as **don't** and **can't** are more informal than the full, unabbreviated versions. Think about your audience when deciding which to use.

Apostrophes of possession

Apostrophes can be used to show that something or someone belongs to someone or something else.

- The boy's hands ...
- Betty's sister ...
- The dog's collar ...
- The school's head teacher ...

Note that if the word to which you are adding the apostrophe ends in s you can just add the apostrophe after the s:

The teachers' voices

Mrs Roberts' book

Note that this is a plural: there is more than one teacher.

You can also, when a name ends in s, add an apostrophe and another s:

Mrs Roberts's book

Speech punctuation

- Use speech marks to enclose the words that are spoken.
- Start the speech with a capital letter.
- There is **always** a punctuation mark just before the closing speech marks.
- Use a comma if you are adding who is speaking ...
- ... followed by a lower case letter immediately after the closing speech marks.
- Use a full stop if you are not adding who is speaking.

'Mum, can I have some sweets?' begged Aran.

'It's nearly dinner time,' his mother replied.

'Mum, I want some sweets.'

'I've just told you,' said his mother patiently.

Now try this

There are several **punctuation** errors in this student's writing. Copy and correct it.

'theres nothing I can do said Garys dad.
'are you sure,' Replied Gary.
'idont know what you mean.' Said his dad.
'i think you do'

Avoid too much dialogue in imaginative writing. Focus on full paragraphs of prose to show you understand sentence structures.

Colons, semi-colons, dashes, brackets and ellipses

Punctuation can help you develop your ideas and express yourself clearly.

Semi-colons

You can **link two connected ideas** with a semi-colon instead of a conjunction.

For example, you could write:

> Education is a privilege and it should be treasured.

Or you could write:

> Education is a privilege; it should be treasured.

Dashes and brackets

These can be used to **add** extra, but not entirely necessary, information to a sentence. Before using brackets or dashes, ask yourself: Is this important information? Or would my writing be better without it?

Dashes can be used in **pairs** to add information mid-sentence:

> Several years ago – though I can't remember exactly when – my sister moved to Scotland.

Single dashes can be used at the end of a sentence, to suggest a pause before an afterthought:

> I'm sure there was a reason – but no one ever told me what it was.

3 **Brackets** must be used in **pairs**:

> The house (which my mother hated) was near the sea.

Colons

Use a colon to **introduce an example**:

> Students have two choices: work hard or fail.

Or to **introduce a list**:

> You will need: a pen, a pencil, a ruler and an eraser.

Or to **introduce an explanation**:

> English is my favourite subject: I love creative writing.

Ellipses

You can use an ellipsis in **dialogue** to suggest a **dramatic pause** or to show someone falling into **silence**:

> 'I don't know where I...'
> He looked mystified.

> 'And the winner is...'

Using an ellipsis to suggest tension in descriptive writing can seem clichéd. Instead, create tension through your choice of language and sentence structure:

> He opened the door and realised to his horror that the room was completely empty...

> He opened the door. The room was completely empty.

Now try this

Answer the following questions using the information on this page.

1 What punctuation could you use to introduce an explanation?
2 What could you use instead of a conjunction to link two connected ideas?
3 When might you use a pair of dashes?

Putting it into practice

For **both papers** you will need to show you can use a range of punctuation accurately. Look at the **Paper 2** exam-style question below and read the extracts from two students' answers.

Worked example

5 'It is important for children and their parents to spend time together and share a hobby.'
Write an article for your school magazine in which you explain your point of view on this statement. **(40 marks)**

Punctuation

In each of the writing tasks you need to show you can:

- ✓ punctuate accurately
- ✓ use a full range of punctuation
- ✓ use punctuation effectively to express yourself clearly.

Sample answer extract

My dad and I are both mad about football, its something we could'nt live without and it really brings us together. I love playing it and watching it whether its a few friends having a kickabout at lunchtime or an FA Cup final on the telly. There are lots of reasons it means so much to me but the main one is that my dad loves football so its something we have in common. He does'nt play football but we can spend hours talking about it, who scored, who didnt score who should be playing and who should be dropped.

✗ Incorrectly placed apostrophes.

✗ Comma splice. This should either be a semi-colon or a full stop followed by a new sentence.

✗ Missing apostrophe.

✗ Missed opportunity for a colon to introduce a list.

✗ Missing comma separating items in a list.

The use of full stops is **generally** accurate.

Improved sample answer

Spending time with my mother is something I treasure. It gives us the chance to catch up properly, to share worries, to understand each other better; it's time I wouldn't give up for all the world. It was Mum who first taught me to ride. I remember that first time: Mum lifted me into the saddle – which seemed as high as the moon – and helped me find my balance.

Without the support and understanding that parents can offer, growing up can be a bewildering and lonely experience. Yet how can children and parents understand one another if they spend all their time apart?

These days, Mum and I go trekking every weekend. It's these afternoons that ensure our relationship stays open, trusting and strong.

The full stops in the improved answer are **completely** accurate.

✓ Correct use of apostrophe.

✓ Commas, semi-colons and colons are all used accurately. Notice how the commas separate items in a list, the colon is used to introduce an explanation, and the semi-colon acts like a full stop.

Always remember to check your punctuation – especially full stops – for accuracy.

Now try this

Write the first paragraph of your answer to the above exam-style question. Aim to use a range of punctuation accurately, including commas, apostrophes, colons and semi-colons.

Had a look ☐ Nearly there ☐ Nailed it! ☐

Common spelling errors 1

For **both papers** you will need to show you can spell correctly. There are some spelling mistakes that occur again and again in students' exam responses. Learn how to avoid making them.

Would have, could have, should have

Students often use **would of** or **should of** or **could of** when they should use **would have**, **should have**, or **could have**. For example:

✗ Global warming could of been prevented. We should of started thinking more carefully about the environment long ago.

This is what should have been written: could **have** ✓ should **have** ✓

Our, are

Students often confuse *our* and *are*:

- **our** means *belonging to us*
- **are** is from the verb *to be*.

✗ We should always look after are bodies. They our precious.

This is what should have been written: **our** bodies ✓ **are** precious ✓

There, their, they're

Make sure you learn these spellings:

- **their** means belonging to **them**
- **there** is used to describe the position of something (**It's over there**) and in the phrases **There is** or **There are**
- **they're** is an abbreviation of **they are**.

✗ Their were three people at the table, all eating there dinner.

✓ ~~Their~~ There were three people at the table, all eating ~~there~~ their dinner.

Affect, effect

One of these is a verb, and the other a noun:

- **affect** is a verb
- **effect** is usually used as a noun.

For example, you may have been **affected** by a problem. But the problem had an **effect** on you. If the word has got **an** or **the** in front of it, it's a noun, so it's spelt **effect**.

-ly or -ley?

When you add *-ly* to a word, make sure you don't swap the 'l' and the 'e':

definite + ly = definitely

bravley ✗ bravely ✓

safley ✗ safely ✓

rudley ✗ rudely ✓

There are **very few** words which end in -ley. Learn these examples: alley, medley, trolley, valley.

Its or it's?

It's is an abbreviation of **it is**. **Its** means belonging to **it**.

✗ Its the end of it's life.

✓ ~~Its~~ It's the end of ~~it's~~ its life.

Now try this

Look back at the last five pieces of writing you have completed. Have you made any of these common spelling errors? If so, correct them.

Common spelling errors 2

Your and you're

Learn the difference between these two words:

- **your** means **belonging to you**
- **you're** is an abbreviation of **you are**.

✗ Your having the time of you're life.

✓ ~~Your~~/You're having the time of ~~you're~~/your life.

Remember: **a lot** is two words. **Alot of people love chocolate** is wrong, but **A lot of people love chocolate** is correct.

We're, wear, were and where

Make sure you are familiar with each of these:

- **we're** is an abbreviation of **we are**
- **wear** is a verb referring to clothing – e.g. **What are you wearing tonight?**
- **were** is the past tense of are – e.g. **they are**, they were
- **where** is a question word referring to place – e.g. **Where are we going?**

✗ Wear we're you? Were leaving now.

✓ ~~Wear we're~~/Where were you? ~~Were~~/We're leaving now.

Two, too, to

Getting these words wrong is quite a common error:

- **to** indicates place, direction or position – e.g. **I went to Spain.**
- **too** means **also** or an **excessive amount** – e.g. **I went too far.**
- **two** is a number.

✗ It's to difficult to get too the highest level.

✓ It's ~~to~~/too difficult to get ~~too~~/to the highest level.

Of, off

The easiest way to remember the difference is by listening to the sound of the word you want to use:

- **of** is pronounced ov
- **off** rhymes with cough.

✗ He jumped of the top off the wall.

✓ He jumped ~~of~~/off the top ~~off~~/of the wall.

Past, passed

Aim to get these two right:

- **passed** is the past tense of the verb to pass – e.g. **He passed all his GCSEs.**
- **past** refers to time that has gone by, or position – e.g. **That's all in the past; He ran past the school.**

✗ She past out at ten passed six.

✓ She ~~past~~/passed out at ten ~~passed~~/past six.

Who's and whose

Whose is a question word referring to belonging, e.g. **Whose book is this?**

Who's is an abbreviation of **who is.**

✗ Whose wearing who's coat?

✓ ~~Whose~~/Who's wearing ~~who's~~/whose coat?

Now try this

There are **nine** spelling errors in this student's writing. Copy and correct it.

I saw Annabel walk passed wearing you're shoes. She was carrying you're bag to. I don't know who's coat she had on but it had too stripes across the back. She stopped and took it of. I don't know were she was going or what she was up two. It was very strange.

Common spelling errors 3

Some of the most frequently misspelt are listed below. Make sure you learn how to spell these words properly.

amusement
argument

Notice the 'e' here but not here.

opportunity
disappoint
embarrassing
beginning
occasionally
difficult
disappear
possession
recommend

Check which letters are **doubled** and which are not.

privilege
definitely
separately
conscious
conscience
experience
independence

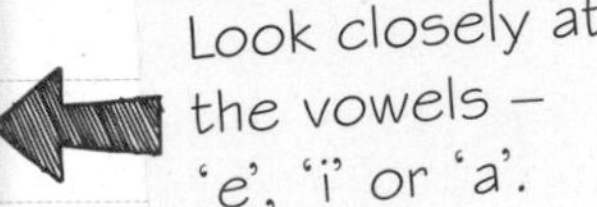
Look closely at the vowels – 'e', 'i' or 'a'.

business

Silent 'i' in the middle.

believe weird

'ei' or 'ie'?

rhythm

Two 'h's, but no vowels.

decision

Get the 'c' and the 's' round the right way.

grateful

Not greatful; **grat**eful = to show **grat**itude.

Learning correct spellings

Find a hidden word. Look for words hidden within the word you are learning. For example, **separate** becomes much easier to remember when you notice that there's a **rat** in the middle of it:

sep a **rat** e

Say what you see. Say the word aloud, breaking it up into syllables and pronouncing them as they are written. For example, read these syllables aloud:

def / in / ite / ly

Now try this

Test yourself on these spellings. Learn any which you get wrong, then you could ask a friend or family member to re-test you.

Proofreading

For **both papers** it is essential that you leave time at the end of the exam to **check your work**. It could make all the difference.

What kinds of mistakes do you make?

Here's a list of common errors:

- spelling mistakes
- missing or incorrect punctuation
- grammatical errors such as misused, repeated or missing words.

Most people make **all three** kinds of mistakes, especially when they are writing in a hurry.

Ideally, you should check your work through three times:

- once for spelling
- once for punctuation
- once to check it makes clear sense, with no misused, repeated or missing words.

You **will** have made mistakes. Aim to find **five or more** in each of your answers.

Alarm bells

Train your proofreading brain to ring an alarm bell whenever you come across **their, there, its, it's** or any one of the common spelling errors that everyone makes. When the alarm rings, **stop!** Double check that you've used the correct spelling.

How to check your spelling

If you know you've spelt a word incorrectly, but you're not sure of the correct spelling, try it three or four different ways in the margin. Pick the one that looks right:

seperatly ✗ separetly ✗
separately ✓ separatley ✗

Reading your work backwards – from bottom to top, right to left – stops you thinking about the meaning of your writing and makes you focus on spelling.

Checking for sense: tips

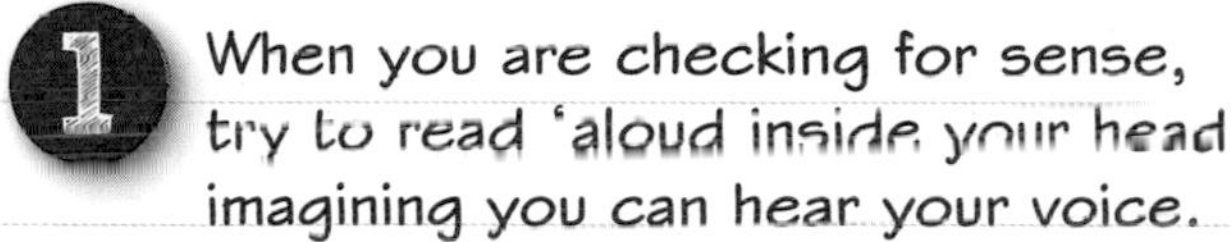

1. When you are checking for sense, try to read 'aloud inside your head' imagining you can hear your voice.

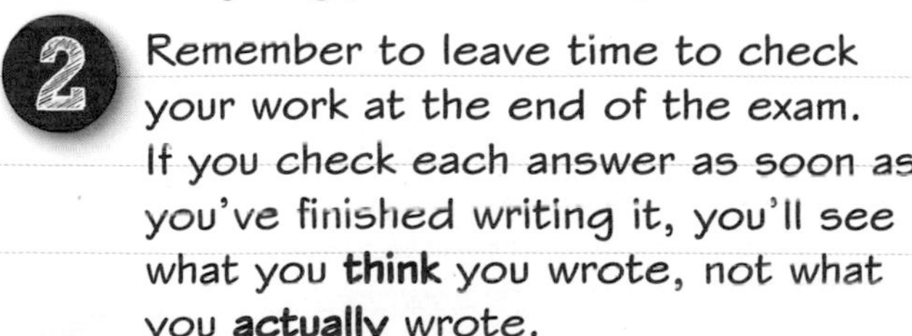

2. Remember to leave time to check your work at the end of the exam. If you check each answer as soon as you've finished writing it, you'll see what you **think** you wrote, not what you **actually** wrote.

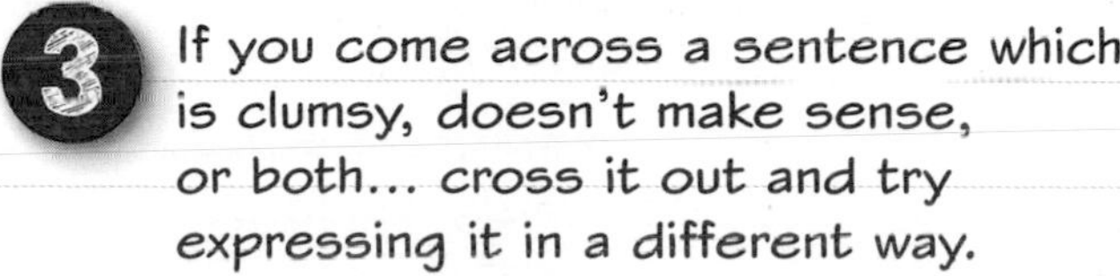

3. If you come across a sentence which is clumsy, doesn't make sense, or both... cross it out and try expressing it in a different way.

Putting it right

Accurate writing achieves higher marks than neat writing. So, if you find a mistake – whether it's a word, a sentence, or a whole paragraph – **cross it out**. Put **one neat line** through the mistake and add your correction by:

- using one of these ⁄ ~~to make a mistake~~ (to guide the reader)
- or by using an asterisk.*

If you forget to start a new paragraph, use // to mark where one paragraph ends and the next one begins.

* To tell the reader to read this bit next.

Now try this

Look over five pieces of writing you have produced recently. How many mistakes can you find?

Putting it into practice

For **both papers** your writing needs to be as **accurate** as possible. You need to check your work for **errors** in **spelling, punctuation** and **grammar**. Look at the **Paper 2** exam-style question below and read the extracts from two students' answers.

Worked example

5 'Every teenager should have a part-time job. It teaches them the value of money and prepares them for life.'

Write a letter to a broadsheet newspaper in which you argue for or against this statement. **(40 marks)**

Proofreading

For both papers you should:

- ✓ spend about 5 minutes carefully checking your work
- ✓ correct any spelling errors
- ✓ correct any punctuation errors
- ✓ ensure your writing makes clear sense.

Finding and changing errors could really improve your answer.

Sample answer extract

Everyone says GCSEs have got easyer but they dont realise how difficult they are and how how much work we have to do at school. There just isn't time to do all the school work and have a part-time job, we need some to rest and and enjoy ourselves. On an avarage day I go to school for six hours, get home and do an hour or two of homework. I could go out to work in the evenings but Id get home late and be realy tired at school the next day which would make it realy dificult to concentrate at school the next day.

Make sure you spend some time checking your answers. The second sentence:

- is clumsily written
- has errors
- is not clear in its meaning.

✗ Spelling errors

✗ Punctuation errors

Improved sample answer

Working for my money has certainly taught me its value. For example, when I was younger and wanted to buy something, I had to pester my mum.* Now, because I've e~~l~~arned my money, ~~I can buy what I want. Because of that I always make sure I know I want what I'm buying.~~ I make very sure I'm not wasting my money on something I ~~dont~~ don't really need.

* Usually, once I'd got it, I would realise that I didn't really want it anymore.

✓ Spelling and punctuation errors both corrected.

It's fine to cross out clumsy writing and add in something that is easier to read and understand.

✓ The additional explanation effectively reinforces the argument.

Now try this

Look back at a piece of writing you have completed recently. Check it three times, looking for:

- sentences that are clumsily written or unclear
- missing or repeated words
- spelling mistakes
- punctuation errors.

Aim to find at least **five** mistakes and correct them.

Cut along the dotted lines and staple the texts together to make your own handy anthology. Make sure you keep it safe with your Revision Guide.

SOURCE 1

This extract is from the opening of a novel by Daphne du Maurier. It was published in 1938. In this section the narrator is dreaming of a home she once lived in, Manderley.

Rebecca

Last night I dreamt I went to Manderley again. It seemed to me I stood by the iron gate leading to the drive, and for a while I could not enter, for the way was barred to me. There was a padlock and chain upon the gate. I called in my dream to the lodge-keeper, and had no answer, and peering closer through the rusted spokes of the gate I saw that the lodge was uninhabited.

No smoke came from the chimney, and the little lattice[1] windows gaped forlorn. Then, like all dreamers, I was possessed of a sudden with supernatural powers and passed like a spirit through the barrier before me. The drive wound away in front of me, twisting and turning as it had always done, but as I advanced I was aware that a change had come upon it; it was narrow and unkempt, not the drive that we had known. At first I was puzzled and did not understand, and it was only when I bent my head to avoid the low swinging branch of a tree that I realized what had happened. Nature had come into her own again and, little by little, in her stealthy, insidious[2] way had encroached upon the drive with long, tenacious[3] fingers. The woods, always a menace even in the past, had triumphed in the end. They crowded, dark and uncontrolled, to the borders of the drive. The beeches with white, naked limbs leant close to one another, their branches intermingled in a strange embrace, making a vault above my head like the archway of a church. And there were other trees as well, trees that I did not recognize, squat oaks and tortured elms that straggled cheek by jowl[4] with the beeches, and had thrust themselves out of the quiet earth, along with monster shrubs and plants, none of which I remembered.

The drive was a ribbon now, a thread of its former self, with gravel surface gone, and choked with grass and moss. The trees had thrown out low branches, making an impediment to progress; the gnarled roots looked like skeleton claws. Scattered here and again amongst this jungle growth I would recognize shrubs that had been landmarks in our time, things of culture and grace, hydrangeas whose blue heads had been famous. No hand had checked their progress, and they had gone native now, rearing to monster height without a bloom, black and ugly as the nameless parasites that grew beside them.

On and on, now east now west, wound the poor thread that once had been our drive. Sometimes I thought it lost, but it appeared again, beneath a fallen tree perhaps, or struggling on the other side of a muddied ditch created by the winter rains. I had not thought the way so long. Surely the miles had multiplied, even as the trees had done, and this path led but to a labyrinth[5], some choked wilderness, and not to the house at all. I came upon it suddenly; the approach masked by the unnatural growth of a vast shrub that spread in all directions, and I stood, my heart thumping in my breast, the strange prick of tears behind my eyes.

There was Manderley, our Manderley, secretive and silent as it had always been, the grey stone shining in the moonlight of my dream, the mullioned[6] windows reflecting the green lawns and the terrace. Time could not wreck the perfect symmetry of those walls, nor the site itself, a jewel in the hollow of a hand.

The terrace sloped to the lawns, and the lawns stretched to the sea, and turning I could see the sheet of silver placid under the moon, like a lake undisturbed by wind or storm. No waves would come to ruffle this dream water, and no bulk of cloud, wind-driven from the west, obscure the clarity of this pale sky. I turned again to the house, and though it stood inviolate[7], untouched, as though we ourselves had left but yesterday, I saw that the garden had obeyed the jungle law, even as the woods had done. The rhododendrons stood fifty feet high, twisted and entwined with bracken, and they had entered into alien marriage with a host of nameless shrubs, poor, bastard things that clung about their roots as though conscious of their spurious[8] origin. A lilac had mated with a copper beech, and to bind them yet more closely to one another the malevolent ivy, always an enemy to grace, had thrown her tendrils[9] about the pair and made them prisoners. Ivy held prior place in this lost garden, the long strands crept across the lawns, and soon would encroach upon the house itself. There was another plant too, some half breed from the woods, whose seed had been scattered long ago beneath the trees and then forgotten, and now, marching in unison with the ivy, thrust its ugly form like a giant rhubarb towards the soft grass where the daffodils had blown.

Nettles were everywhere, the vanguard of the army. They choked the terrace, they sprawled about the paths, they leant, vulgar and lanky, against the very windows of the house. They made indifferent sentinels[10], for in many places their ranks had been broken by the rhubarb plant, and they lay with crumpled heads and listless stems, making a pathway for the rabbits. I left the drive and went on to the terrace, for the nettles were no barrier to me, a dreamer. I walked enchanted, and nothing held me back.

1: **Lattice:** a pattern of diamond shapes
2: **Insidious:** slow and harmful
3: **Tenacious:** keeping a tight hold
4: **Cheek by jowl:** close together
5: **Labyrinth:** maze
6: **Mullioned windows:** windows with vertical bars between the panes of glass
7: **Inviolate:** injury-free
8: **Spurious:** illegitimate, unlawful
9: **Tendrils:** thread like parts of a climbing plant
10: **Sentinels:** guards

SOURCES

Cut along the dotted lines and staple the texts together to make your own handy anthology. Make sure you keep it safe with your Revision Guide.

SOURCE 2

This extract is from the first chapter of a novel by Harper Lee. It is set in Alabama in the United States in the 1930s. The narrator is called Scout; she is Jem's sister.

To Kill a Mockingbird

Maycomb was an old town, but it was a tired old town when I first knew it. In rainy weather the streets turned to red slop; grass grew on the sidewalks, the courthouse sagged in the square. Somehow, it was hotter then: a black dog suffered on a summer's day; bony mules[1] hitched to Hoover carts[2] flicked flies in the sweltering shade of the live oaks on the square. Men's stiff collars wilted by nine in the morning. Ladies bathed before noon, after their three-o'clock naps, and by nightfall were like soft teacakes with frostings of sweat and sweet talcum.

People moved slowly then. They ambled across the square, shuffled in and out of the stores around it, took their time about everything. A day was twenty-four hours long but seemed longer. There was no hurry, for there was nowhere to go, nothing to buy and no money to buy it with, nothing to see outside the boundaries of Maycomb County. But it was a time of vague optimism for some of the people: Maycomb County had recently been told that it had nothing to fear but fear itself.

We lived on the main residential street in town—Atticus, Jem and I, plus Calpurnia our cook. Jem and I found our Father satisfactory: he played with us, read to us, and treated us with courteous[3] detachment.

Calpurnia was something else again. She was all angles and bones; she was nearsighted; she squinted; her hand was wide as a bed slat and twice as hard. She was always ordering me out of the kitchen, asking me why I couldn't behave as well as Jem when she knew he was older, and calling me home when I wasn't ready to come. Our battles were epic and one-sided. Calpurnia always won, mainly because Atticus 'ways took her side. She had been with us ever since Jem was born, and I had felt her tyrannical presence as long as I could remember.

Our mother died when I was two, so I never felt her absence. She was a Graham from Montgomery—Atticus met her when he was first elected to the state legislature. He was middle-aged then, she was fifteen years his junior. Jem was the product of their first year of marriage; four years later I was born, and two years later our mother died from a sudden heart attack. They said it ran in her family. I did not miss her, but I think Jem did. He remembered her clearly, and sometimes in the middle of a game he would sigh at length, then go off and play by himself behind the car-house. When he was like that, I knew better than to bother him.

When I was almost six and Jem was nearly ten, our summertime boundaries (within calling distance of Calpurnia) were Mrs. Henry Lafayette Dubose's house two doors to the north of us, and the Radley Place three doors to the south. We were never tempted to break them. The Radley Place was inhabited by an unknown entity[4] the mere description of whom was enough to make us behave for days on end; Mrs. Dubose was plain hell.

That was the summer Dill came to us.

Early one morning as we were beginning our day's play in the backyard, Jem and I heard something next door in Miss Rachel Haverford's collard[5] patch. We went to the wire fence to see if there was a puppy—Miss Rachel's rat terrier was expecting—instead we found someone sitting looking at us. Sitting down, he wasn't much higher than the collards. We stared at him until he spoke:

"Hey."

"Hey yourself," said Jem pleasantly.

"I'm Charles Baker Harris," he said. "I can read."

"So what?" I said.

"I just thought you'd like to know I can read. You got anything needs readin' I can do it...."

"How old are you," asked Jem, "four-and-a-half?"

"Goin' on seven."

"Shoot no wonder, then," said Jem, jerking his thumb at me.

"Scout yonder's been readin' ever since she was born, and she ain't even started to school yet. You look right puny for goin' on seven."

"I'm little but I'm old," he said.

Jem brushed his hair back to get a better look. "Why don't you come over, Charles Baker Harris?" he said. "Lord, what a name."

"'s not any funnier'n yours. Aunt Rachel says your name's Jeremy Atticus Finch."

Jem scowled. "I'm big enough to fit mine," he said. "Your name's longer'n you are. Bet it's a foot longer."

"Folks call me Dill," said Dill, struggling under the fence.

1: **Mules:** animals that are a cross between a donkey and a horse
2: **Hoover carts:** a cart made using the wheels from a car
3: **Courteous:** polite
4: **Entity:** being, body
5: **Collard:** a green, leafy vegetable

Cut along the dotted lines and staple the texts together to make your own handy anthology. Make sure you keep it safe with your Revision Guide.

SOURCE 3

This extract is from a novel by Beryl Bainbridge. It is set on the ill-fated Titanic. In this section, the ship is sinking and the passengers are in grave danger.

Every Man for Himself

And now, the moment was almost upon us. The stern began to lift from the water. Guggenheim and his valet[1] played mountaineers, going hand over hand up the rail. The hymn turned ragged; ceased altogether. The musicians scrambled upwards, the spike of the cello scraping the deck. Clinging to the rung of the ladder I tried to climb to the roof but there was such a sideways slant that I waved like a flag on a pole. I thought I must make a leap for it and turned to look for Hopper. Something, some inner voice urged me to glance below and I saw Scurra again, one arm hooked through the rail to steady himself. I raised my hand in greeting – then the water, first slithering, then tumbling, gushed us apart.

As the ship staggered and tipped, a great volume of water flowed in over the submerged bows[2] and tossed me like a cork to the roof. Hopper was there too. My fingers touched some kind of bolt near the ventilation grille and I grabbed it tight. I filled my lungs with air and fixed my eyes on the blurred horizon, determined to hang on until I was sure I could float free rather than be swilled back and forth in a maelstrom[3]. I wouldn't waste my strength in swimming, not yet, for I knew the ship was now my enemy and if I wasn't vigilant would drag me with her to the grave. I waited for the next slithering dip and when it came and the waves rushed in and swept me higher, I released my grip and let myself be carried away, over the tangle of ropes and wires and davits[4], clear of the rails and out into the darkness. I heard the angry roaring of the dying ship, the deafening cacophony as she stood on end and all her guts tore loose. I choked on soot and cringed beneath the sparks dancing like fire-flies as the forward funnel broke and smashed the sea in two. I thought I saw Hopper's face but one eye was ripped away and he gobbled like a fish on the hook. I was sucked under, as I knew I would be, down, down, and still I waited, waited until the pull slackened – then I struck out with all my strength.

I don't know how long I swam under that lidded sea – time had stopped with my breath – and just as it seemed as if my lungs would burst the blackness paled and I kicked to the surface. I had thought I was entering paradise, for I was alive and about to breathe again, and then I heard the cries of souls in torment and believed myself in hell. Dear God! Those voices! *Father… Father… For the love of Christ… Help me, for pity's sake!… Where is my son.* Some called for their mothers, some on the Lord, some to die quickly, a few to be saved. The lamentations[5] rang through the frosty air and touched the stars; my own mouth opened in a silent howl of grief. The cries went on and on, trembling, lingering – and God forgive me, but I wanted them to end. In all that ghastly night it was the din of the dying that chilled the most. Presently, the voices grew fainter, ceased – yet still I heard them, as though the drowned called to one another in a ghostly place where none could follow. Then silence fell, and that was the worst sound of all. There was no trace of the *Titanic*. All that remained was a grey veil of vapour[6] drifting above the water.

Gradually I grew accustomed to the darkness and made out a boat some distance away. Summoning up all my strength I swam closer; it was a collapsible, wrong side up and sagging in the sea. I tried to climb on to the gunwale[7] but the occupants gazed through me and offered no assistance; they might have been dead men for all the life in their eyes. Swimming round to the far side, I commandeered a bobbing barrel, and, mounting it like a horse, hand-paddled to the stern and flung myself aboard.

1: **Valet:** male servant
2: **Bows:** the front end of a ship
3: **Maelstrom:** a powerful whirlpool
4: **Davits:** small cranes
5: **Lamentations:** sorrowful cries
6: **Vapour:** mist
7: **Gunwale:** the side of a boat

SOURCES

Cut along the dotted lines and staple the texts together to make your own handy anthology. Make sure you keep it safe with your Revision Guide.

SOURCE 4

This extract is from the opening of a novel by Kathryn Stockett. Published in 2009, the novel describes the lives of black maids working in white homes in the 1960s, in Jackson, Mississippi, in the United States.

The Help

Mae Mobley was born on a early Sunday morning in August, 1960. A church baby we like to call it. Taking care a white babies, that's what I do, along with all the cooking and the cleaning. I done raised seventeen kids in my lifetime. I know how to get them babies to sleep, stop crying, and go in the toilet bowl before they mamas even get out a bed in the morning.

But I ain't never seen a baby yell like Mae Mobley Leefolt. First day I walk in the door, there she be, red-hot and hollering with the colic[1], fighting that bottle like it's a rotten turnip. Miss Leefolt, she look terrified at her own child. 'What am I doing wrong? Why can't I stop it?'

It? That was my first hint: something is wrong with this situation.

So I took that pink, screaming baby in my arms. Bounced her on my hip to get the gas moving and it didn't take two minutes fore Baby Girl stopped her crying, got to smiling up at me like she do. But Miss Leefolt, she don't pick up her own baby for the rest a the day. I seen plenty a womens get the baby blues[2] after they done birthing. I reckon I thought that's what it was.

Here's something about Miss Leefolt: she not just frowning all the time, she skinny. Her legs is so spindly, she look like she done growed em last week. Twenty-three years old and she lanky as a fourteen-year-old boy. Even her hair is thin, brown, see-through. She try to tease it up, but it only make it look thinner. Her face be the same shape as that red devil on the redhot candy box[3], pointy chin and all. Fact, her whole body be so full a sharp knobs and corners, it's no wonder she can't soothe that baby. Babies like fat. Like to bury they face up in you armpit and go to sleep. They like big fat legs too. That I know.

By the time she a year old, Mae Mobley following me around everwhere I go. Five o'clock would come round and she'd be hanging on my Dr. Scholl shoe, dragging over the floor, crying like I weren't never coming back. Miss Leefolt, she'd narrow up her eyes at me like I done something wrong, unhitch that crying baby off my foot. I reckon that's the risk you run, letting somebody else raise you chilluns.

Mae Mobley two years old now. She got big brown eyes and honey-colour curls. But the bald spot in the back of her hair kind a throw things off. She get the same wrinkle between her eyebrows when she worried, like her mama. They kind a favour except Mae Mobley so fat. She ain't gone be no beauty queen. I think it bother Miss Leefolt, but Mae Mobley my special baby.

I lost my own boy, Treelore, right before I started waiting on Miss Leefolt. He was twenty-four years old. The best part of a person's life. It just wasn't enough time living in this world.

He had him a little apartment over on Foley Street. Seeing a real nice girl name Frances and I spec they was gone get married, but he was slow bout things like that. Not cause he looking for something better, just cause he the thinking kind. Wore big glasses and reading all the time. He even start writing his own book, bout being a coloured man living and working in Mississippi. Law, that made me proud. But one night he working late at the Scanlon-Taylor mill, lugging two-by-fours[4] to the truck, splinters slicing all the way through the glove. He too small for that kind a work, too skinny, but he needed the job. He was tired. It was raining. He slip off the loading dock, fell down on the drive. Tractor trailer didn't see him and crushed his lungs fore he could move. By the time I found out, he was dead.

That was the day my whole world went black. Air look black, sun look black. I laid up in bed and stared at the black walls a my house. Minny came ever day to make sure I was still breathing, feed me food to keep me living. Took three months fore I even look out the window, see if the world still there. I was surprise to see the world didn't stop just cause my boy did.

Five months after the funeral, I lifted myself up out a bed. I put on my white uniform and put my little gold cross back around my neck and I went to wait on Miss Leefolt cause she just have her baby girl. But it weren't too long before I seen something in me had changed. A bitter seed was planted inside a me. And I just didn't feel so accepting anymore.

1: **Colic:** a kind of stomach ache that babies typically get
2: **Baby blues:** depression after having a baby
3: **Redhot candy box:** Red Hot is a brand of candy (sweets)
4: **Two-by-fours:** wooden planks

Cut along the dotted lines and staple the texts together to make your own handy anthology. Make sure you keep it safe with your Revision Guide.

SOURCE 5a

Sir Thomas Fowell Buxton (1786–1845) was a humanitarian who reviewed the state of prisons in the early nineteenth century, and who pushed for prison reform and to reform criminal law.

T.F. Buxton on the state of the Prisons, 1818

The prisoner, after his commitment is made out, is handcuffed to a file or perhaps a dozen wretched persons in a similar situation, and marched through the streets, sometimes a considerable distance, followed by a crowd of impudent and insulting boys, exposed to the gaze and to the stare of every passenger: the moment he enters prison, irons are hammered on to him; then is he cast into the midst of a compound of all that is disgusting and depraved. At night he is locked up in a narrow cell, with perhaps half a dozen of the worst thieves in London, or as many vagrants[1], whose rags are alive, and in actual motion with vermin[2]: he may find himself in bed, and in bodily contact, between a robber and a murderer; or between a man with a foul disease on one side, and one with an infectious disorder on the other. He may spend his days deprived of free air and wholesome exercise. He may be prohibited from following the handicraft on which the subsistence[3] of his family depends. He may be half-starved for want of food, and clothing and fuel. He may be compelled to mingle with the vilest of mankind, and in self-defence, to adopt their habits, their language and their sentiments; he may become a villain by actual compulsion[4]. His health must be impaired, and may be ruined, by filth and contagion[5]; and as for his morals, purity itself could not continue pure, if exposed for any length of time to the society with which he must associate.

His trial may be long protracted; he may be imprisoned on suspicion, and pine in jail while his family is starving out of it, without any opportunity of removing that suspicion, and this for a whole year: if acquitted, he may be dismissed from jail without a shilling in his pocket, and without the means of returning home; if convicted, beyond the sentence awarded by the law, he may be exposed to the most intolerable hardships, and these may amount to no less than the destruction of his life now, and his soul forever. And in the violation of his rights, you equally abandon your own interest. He is instructed in no useful branch of employment by which he may earn an honest livelihood by honest labour. You have forbidden him to repent[6] and to reflect, by withholding from him every opportunity of reflection and repentance. Seclusion from the world has been only a closer intercourse with its very worst miscreants[7]; his mind has lain waste and barren for every weed to take root in; he is habituated to idleness, reconciled to filth, and familiarised with crime. You give him leisure, and for the employment of that leisure you give him tutors in every branch of iniquity[8]. You have taken no pious[9] pains to turn him from the error of his ways, and to save his soul alive. You have not cherished the latent seeds of virtue, you have not profited by the opportunity of awakening remorse for his past misconduct. His Saviour's awful name becomes, indeed, familiar to his lips, because he learns to use it, to give zest to his conversation and vigour to his execrations[10]; but all that Saviour's office, His tenderness, and compassion, and mercy to the returning sinner, are topics of which he learns no more than the beasts which perish. In short, by the greatest possible degree of misery, you produce the greatest possible degree of wickedness; you convert an act, perhaps of indiscretion[11], into a settled taste and propensity to vice[12]; receiving him, because he is too bad for society, you return him to the world impaired in health, debased in intellect, and corrupted in principles.

1: **Vagrants:** people without homes or jobs
2: **Vermin:** wild animals that carry disease, like rats
3: **Subsistence:** survival
4: **Compulsion:** obligation, necessity
5: **Contagion:** disease
6: **Repent:** say sorry
7: **Miscreants:** people who behave badly
8: **Iniquity:** immoral or bad behaviour
9: **Pious:** serious
10: **Execrations:** curses
11: **Indiscretion:** mistake
12: **Vice:** immoral or wicked behaviour

Cut along the dotted lines and staple the texts together to make your own handy anthology. Make sure you keep it safe with your Revision Guide.

21st

SOURCE 5b

This source is an article from a newspaper discussing the effectiveness of prisons.

Prison doesn't work 50% of the time, so why do we keep sending people there?

The *Mirror*, 24 June 2014

By Anna Leach

If something didn't work 50% of the time, would you keep doing it?

One in every two criminals leaving prison will commit another crime within one year of walking out the prison gates.

If the aim of prison is to stop people committing crimes, it's not really working.

- 47% of offenders leaving prison reoffend within one year
- 58% of prisoners on short sentences reoffend within a year of leaving jail
- 70% of under-18s given a prison sentence reoffend within 12 months

What works better?

From a cold look at the statistics, this does not look like a successful way to reduce crime. Especially not for young offenders, and especially not for people on short-term sentences.

Here are some things that work slightly better.

Community sentences reduce reoffending by 6%

Okay, they're seen as a softer option by offenders and by the public, but when people are up in the dock convicted of an imprisonable crime (an indictable offence) they are less likely to end up back in trouble if the judge gives them a community order[1] rather than a prison sentence. In 2010 it pulled reoffending rates for short-term sentences down by 6% from 62% to 56%.

The range in effectiveness depends on the type of custodial sentence[2] that community orders are compared to.

The Ministry of Justice compiled this data by comparing offenders with roughly similar crimes and offence histories and then analyzing the outcomes of their different sentences.

Not sending offenders to prison reduces reoffending by 9%

Simply not sending someone to prison by giving them a suspended sentence instead of jailing them works better too. People who get a suspended sentence are 9% less likely to reoffend than someone who committed a similar crime but got sent to prison.

Getting prisoners to meet their victims reduces reoffending by 14%

Campaigners for restorative justice programmes where offenders engage with the impact of their crime and often meet their victims – say it can reduce reoffending by up to 27%. A government analysis puts the improvement at a more conservative 14%. One important limitation on restorative justice is that it is only considered effective for more minor crimes such as burglary. Restorative justice isn't used for offences like domestic violence, murder or rape.

Why does prison work so badly?

Prison reformers such as the Prison Reform Trust point to demographics of our prisoners as part of the problem: poor education, mental health problems and fewer options for getting their life back on the straight and narrow.

But there are also some simple things that the prison and probation services[3] can do that make things better. Those involve helping prisoners maintain connections with the outside world.

Prison reformers point to the differences between offenders leaving prison after a long time and those leaving prison after a short sentence. Offenders who leave after a longer time get more help readjusting to normal life. Those on shorter sentences don't.

And as we mention above, reoffending rates are significantly higher for people given short term sentences than those given ones over a year.

Support? You can get Job Seekers' Allowance

6 months inside is enough to mean you've lost your job, your flat and possibly your relationship. But because the sentence is comparatively short it means you don't have any support when you come out.

As this Home Office page on support for people leaving prison points out, offenders are eligible for job seekers' allowance. That's about it. Scotland and Wales have more provisions and then the government lists voluntary organizations who can help.

Criminals whose family don't visit them are more likely to reoffend

What else helps? Family visits, according to the Trust. It's something that helps prisoners keep links with normal life while they're inside and so makes it easier to adjust when they get out.

40% of prisoners stated that support from their family would help them stop reoffending in the future. Research indicates that the likelihood of reoffending was 39% higher for prisoners who had not received visits whilst in prison compared to those who had.

We're shelling out for this system – shouldn't it be working better?

Looking at all crimes including offences as minor as TV license infringement and driving offenses the reoffending rate for all crimes and all types of sentences is 27% in a year.

There isn't a magic bullet for stopping criminals committing new crimes, but considering **how expensive it is to keep someone in prison – £36,808** in 2012/13, you'd think there'd be an economic incentive at least to try and improve the system.

1: **Community order:** a sentence served in the community
2: **Custodial sentence:** a prison sentence served in prison
3: **Probation services:** those who supervise offenders in the community

Cut along the dotted lines and staple the texts together to make your own handy anthology. Make sure you keep it safe with your Revision Guide.

SOURCE 6a

Mary Seacole (1805–1881) worked as a nurse in the Crimean War, which lasted from 1853 to 1856. Crimea is a peninsula on the northern coast of the Black Sea, near Ukraine and Russia. This extract is taken from the end of her account of her experiences there.

Wonderful Adventures of Mrs. Seacole in Many Lands

I DID not return to England by the most direct route, but took the opportunity of seeing more of men and manners in yet other lands. Arrived in England at last, we set to work bravely at Aldershott to retrieve our fallen fortunes, and stem off the ruin originated in the Crimea, but all in vain; and at last defeated by fortune, but not I think disgraced, we were obliged to capitulate[1] on very honourable conditions. In plain truth, the old Crimean firm of Seacole and Day was dissolved finally, and its partners had to recommence the world anew. And so ended our campaign. One of us started only the other day for the Antipodes[2], while the other is ready to take any journey to any place where a stout heart and two experienced hands may be of use.

Perhaps it would be right if I were to express more shame and annoyance than I really feel at the pecuniarily[3] disastrous issue of my Crimean adventures, but I cannot – I really cannot. When I would try and feel ashamed of myself for being poor and helpless, I only experience a glow of pride at the other and more pleasing events of my career; when I think of the few whom I failed to pay in full (and so far from blaming me some of them are now my firmest friends), I cannot help remembering also the many who profess themselves indebted to me.

Let me, in as few words as possible, state the results of my Crimean campaign. To be sure, I returned from it shaken in health. I came home wounded, as many others did. Few constitutions, indeed, were the better for those winters before Sebastopol[4], and I was too hard worked not to feel their effects; for a little labour fatigues[5] me now – I cannot watch by sick-beds as I could – a week's want of rest quite knocks me up now. Then I returned bankrupt in fortune. Whereas others in my position may have come back to England rich and prosperous, I found myself poor – beggared. So few words can tell what I have lost.

But what have I gained? I should need a volume to describe that fairly; so much is it, and so cheaply purchased by suffering ten times worse than what I have experienced. I have more than once heard people say that they would gladly suffer illness to enjoy the delights of convalescence[6], and so, by enduring a few days' pain, gain the tender love of relatives and sympathy of friends. And on this principle I rejoice in the trials which have borne me such pleasures as those I now enjoy, for wherever I go I am sure to meet some smiling face; every step I take in the crowded London streets may bring me in contact with some friend, forgotten by me, perhaps, but who soon reminds me of our old life before Sebastopol; it seems very long ago now, when I was of use to him and he to me.

Where, indeed, do I not find friends. In omnibuses[7], in river steamboats, in places of public amusement, in quiet streets and courts, where taking short cuts I lose my way oft-times, spring up old familiar faces to remind me of the months spent on Spring Hill. The sentries at Whitehall relax from the discharge of their important duty of guarding nothing to give me a smile of recognition; the very newspaper offices look friendly as I pass them by; busy Printing-house Yard puts on a cheering smile, and the Punch office in Fleet Street sometimes laughs outright. Now, would all this have happened if I had returned to England a rich woman? Surely not.

A few words more ere I bring these egotistical[8] remarks to a close. It is naturally with feelings of pride and pleasure that I allude to the committee recently organized to aid me; and if I indulge in the vanity of placing their names before my readers, it is simply because every one of the following noblemen and gentlemen knew me in the Crimea, and by consenting to assist me now record publicly their opinion of my services there.

1: **Capitulate:** give up
2: **The Antipodes:** Australia and New Zealand
3: **Pecuniarily:** financially
4: **Sebastopol:** a port in Crimea
5: **Fatigues:** tires
6: **Convalescence:** recovery
7: **Omnibuses:** buses
8: **Egotistical:** selfish

SOURCES

Cut along the dotted lines and staple the texts together to make your own handy anthology. Make sure you keep it safe with your Revision Guide.

SOURCE 6b

Captain Robert Falcon Scott (1868–1912) led two expeditions to the Antarctic. The first, from 1901 to 1904 was successful and the expedition made it further south than anyone had done before. The second expedition ended in disaster, and all men perished. These are Captain Scott's final diary entries.

Captain Scott's Diary

1912

Sunday March 18. – My right foot has gone, nearly all the toes – two days ago I was proud possessor of best feet. These are the steps of my downfall. Like an ass I mixed a small spoonful of curry powder with my melted pemmican[1] – it gave me violent indigestion. I lay awake and in pain all night; woke and felt done on the march; foot went and I didn't know it. A very small measure of neglect and have a foot which is not pleasant to contemplate. Bowers takes first place in condition, but there is not much to choose after all. The others are still confident of getting through – or pretend to be – I don't know! We have the last half fill of oil in our primus[2] and a very small quantity of spirit[3] – this alone between us and thirst. The wind is fair for the moment, and that perhaps is a fact to help. The mileage would have seemed ridiculously small on our outward journey.

Monday, March 19. – Lunch. We camped with difficulty last night and were dreadfully cold till after our supper of cold pemmican and biscuit and half a pannikin[4] of cocoa cooked over the spirit. Then, contrary to expectation, we got warm and all slept well. To-day we started in the usual dragging manner. Sledge dreadfully heavy. We are 15 ½ miles from the depôt[5] and ought to get there in three days. What progress! We have two days' food but barely a day's fuel. All our feet are getting bad—Wilson's best, my right foot worst left alright. There is no chance to nurse one's feet till we can get hot food into us. Amputation is the least I can hope for now, but will trouble spread? That is the serious question. The weather doesn't give us a chance – the wind from the N. to N.W.[6] and -40 temp. to-day.

Wednesday, March 21. – Got within 11 miles of depôt Monday night; had to lay up all yesterday in severe blizzard[7]. To-day forlorn hope, Wilson and Bowers going to depot for fuel.

22 and 23. – Blizzard as bad as ever – Wilson and Bowers unable to start – to-morrow last chance – no fuel and only one or two of food left – must be near the end. Having decided it shall be natural – we shall march for the depôt with or without our effects and die in our tracks.

[Thursday] March 29. – Since the 21st we have had a continuous gale from W.S.W. and S.W[8]. We had fuel to make two cups of tea apiece and bare food for two days on 20th. Every day we have been ready to start for our depôt 11 miles away, but outside the door of the tent it remains a scene of whirling drift. I do not think we can hope for any better things now. We shall stick it out to the end, but we are getting weaker, of course, and the end cannot be far.

It seems a pity, but I do not think I can write more.

R. SCOTT.

Last entry.

For God's sake look after our people.

1: **Pemmican:** a concentrated mixture of fat and protein
2: **Primus:** a camping stove (cooker)
3: **Spirit:** fuel
4: **Pannikin:** a small metal drinking cup
5: **Depot:** the 60th camp from the pole
6: **N. to N.W.:** North to North-West (compass point)
7: **Blizzard:** a severe snowstorm with high winds
8: **W.S.W. and S.W.:** West-southwest and South-West (compass points)

Cut along the dotted lines and staple the texts together to make your own handy anthology. Make sure you keep it safe with your Revision Guide.

SOURCE 7a

Susan B. Anthony (1820–1906) was an American woman committed to social equality and a feminist. In the presidential election of 1872, when women did not have the right to vote, she cast an illegal vote and was arrested. This is the speech she gave after her arrest.

On Women's Right to Vote

Friends and fellow citizens: I stand before you tonight under indictment[1] for the alleged crime of having voted at the last presidential election, without having a lawful right to vote. It shall be my work this evening to prove to you that in thus voting, I not only committed no crime, but, instead, simply exercised my citizen's rights, guaranteed to me and all United States citizens by the National Constitution, beyond the power of any state to deny.

The preamble[2] of the Federal Constitution says:

"We, the people of the United States, in order to form a more perfect union, establish justice, insure domestic tranquillity, provide for the common defense, promote the general welfare, and secure the blessings of liberty to ourselves and our posterity[3], do ordain[4] and establish this Constitution for the United States of America."

It was we, the people; not we, the white male citizens; nor yet we, the male citizens; but we, the whole people, who formed the Union. And we formed it, not to give the blessings of liberty, but to secure them; not to the half of ourselves and the half of our posterity, but to the whole people – women as well as men. And it is a downright mockery to talk to women of their enjoyment of the blessings of liberty while they are denied the use of the only means of securing them provided by this democratic-republican government – the ballot[5].

For any state to make sex a qualification that must ever result in the disfranchisement[6] of one entire half of the people, is to pass a bill of attainder[7], or, an ex post facto law[8], and is therefore a violation[9] of the supreme law of the land. By it the blessings of liberty are forever withheld from women and their female posterity.

To them this government has no just powers derived from the consent of the governed. To them this government is not a democracy. It is not a republic. It is an odious aristocracy; a hateful oligarchy[10] of sex; the most hateful aristocracy ever established on the face of the globe; an oligarchy of wealth, where the rich govern the poor. An oligarchy of learning, where the educated govern the ignorant, or even an oligarchy of race, where the Saxon rules the African, might be endured; but this oligarchy of sex, which makes father, brothers, husband, sons, the oligarchs over the mother and sisters, the wife and daughters, of every household - which ordains all men sovereigns, all women subjects, carries dissension[11], discord[12], and rebellion into every home of the nation.

Webster, Worcester, and Bouvier all define a citizen to be a person in the United States, entitled to vote and hold office.

The only question left to be settled now is: Are women persons? And I hardly believe any of our opponents will have the hardihood to say they are not. Being persons, then, women are citizens; and no state has a right to make any law, or to enforce any old law, that shall abridge[13] their privileges or immunities[14]. Hence, every discrimination against women in the constitutions and laws of the several states is today null and void, precisely as is every one against Negroes.

1: **Under indictment:** formally accused
2: **Preamble:** introduction
3: **Posterity:** all future generations
4: **Ordain:** officially order
5: **Ballot:** voting system
6: **Disfranchisement:** removal of rights
7: **Bill of attainder:** a law that declares someone guilty without a trial
8: **Ex post facto law:** a law that makes something illegal that was actually legal at the time it was committed
9: **Violation:** breaking
10: **Oligarchy:** a small group of people in power
11: **Dissension:** disagreement
12: **Discord:** lack of agreement
13: **Abridge:** reduce
14: **Immunities:** protections

SOURCES

Cut along the dotted lines and staple the texts together to make your own handy anthology. Make sure you keep it safe with your Revision Guide.

21st

SOURCE 7b

Flo Henry looks at the history, statistics, facts and opinions connected with voting, and encourages young women to utilise their right to vote in the lead up to the May 2015 election

From Suffragettes to Political Apathy: why it is essential that women exercise their votes

***Lippy*, 3 February 2015**

By Flo Henry

In 1928, after years of peaceful campaigning and militant tactics alike, a group of now-famous, inspirational women called The Suffragettes achieved their goals: women in the UK over the age of 21 were granted the right to vote. For women everywhere this was a remarkable step: they had the opportunity to change society. Emmeline Pankhurst[1] once stated that the only way to create equality is "through giving women political power", which shows the way that these revolutionary feminists expected patriarchal society[2] to change. They saw giving women the power to vote for the political leaders who decided the policies which dramatically affected their lives as fundamental. Today, we still live in a society where men dominate much of the public and political spheres, but women also have the power to change some of the policies that constrain us.

In the 2010 Election, only 64% of women exercised their right to vote, compared to 66% of men, highlighting that although lower voter turnout is a problem facing the UK as a whole, it affects females more greatly. With the May 2015 General Election fast approaching, in a time when politicians and citizens alike are concerned about voter apathy[3], and celebrity Russell Brand – who encourages people not to vote because politics is 'corrupt' – gaining support, it is time to reflect on the values that these important women stood for. Despite public perceptions, voting is the most powerful tool we have to change society, and it is vital that we exercise our right to vote, in order to challenge the dominant power structures which currently influence all of our lives. This is especially true for women. Despite the common assumption that feminism has 'served its time' and is 'no longer relevant' in today's society, there are a number of political issues which purely affect women, and this is something that cannot change unless women go to polling stations[4]. For instance, today, women's sanitary products are taxed as luxury items – providing evidence for the argument that women are grossly underrepresented, and possibly linked to the fact that Parliament is made up of only 22.7% women.

For both genders, it is important to remember that in our current international political system, voting is increasingly making a difference. Things such as the recent Greek election of anti-austerity party Syriza, and the rise of UKIP, The SNP and The Green Party in the UK, show that the amazing thing about politics is that in our democracy, we hold the power to change the political environment. For instance, blind surveys by the website voteforpolicies.org.uk show that 50,000 people polled were unaware of the positions held by each party, highlighting the lack of enthusiasm for politics' power to instigate change. We need to stop our obsession with petty aspects of political leaders, and decide to ignore which politician once smoked Marijuana, or who was once was photographed eating a bacon sandwich. There are more pressing issues. Ultimately, we need to fight for feminism, and against voter apathy in society. The suffragettes were so enthusiastic about the way that politics could change their lives that they spent their lives campaigning for it, some even sacrificing their lives for it. Today, all we have to do is walk to a polling station. Politics affects every aspect of our lives, and we hold the power to influence it.

Want to restore some of the suffragette enthusiasm for the power of politics? Register to vote in the May 2015 General Election now.

1: **Emmeline Pankhurst:** a leader of the Suffragette movement
2: **Patriarchal society:** a society run by men
3: **Apathy:** lack of interest or enthusiasm
4: **Polling stations:** a building where voting takes place

ANSWERS

SECTION A: READING

1. The exam papers explained

The advice required is 'last-minute' so answers should be focused on exam strategy. For example:
- take highlighter pens in different colours for annotation
- stay hydrated
- write the time you should spend on each question in the margins
- keep your answers focused on the question
- breathe slowly and deeply to keep calm.

2. Planning your exam time

1 Paper 1, Question 1 and Paper 2, Question 1
2 Paper 2, Question 4
3 By skim reading the source texts.
4 Stop, take a breath and start again, this time reading more slowly.
5 (a) For both papers: 40 marks for reading.
(b) For both papers: 40 marks for writing.

3. Paper 1 Reading questions 1

Answers should list four things from the text. For example:
- old
- tired
- rainy weather
- streets described as 'red slop'.

4. Paper 1 Reading questions 2

Answers should list three quotations for each viewpoint. For example:

Manderley is presented as a threatening place:
- 'alien marriage'
- 'the jungle law'
- 'made them prisoners'

Manderley is presented as a special place:
- 'There was Manderley, our Manderley, secretive and silent as it had always been'
- 'Time could not wreck the perfect symmetry of those walls'
- 'a jewel in the hollow of a hand'

5. Paper 2 Reading questions 1

- discrimination against women is wrong
- women should be treated equally
- there is only one question left to answer
- women are citizens

6. Paper 2 Reading questions 2

1 Both sources
2 The whole of each source
3 'Compare', 'convey', 'attitudes'
4 'attitudes towards the role of women'
5 About 20 minutes, including about 5 minutes' planning time

7. Skimming for the main idea

For example: The writer has sympathy for the prisoners, who have a very hard time, are treated unfairly and are damaged by the system. The prison service helps neither the prisoners nor society.

8. Annotating the sources

Answers could include the following.
- Choice of word 'vanguard' – represents the power and dominance of the nettles.
- Use of powerful verbs 'choked', 'sprawled', 'broken' – paints a destructive picture of Manderley.
- Use of adjectives 'vulgar', 'lanky', 'crumpled', 'listless' – presents Manderley as a decaying, damaged place.
- Vocabulary with dream-like or fairy tale connotations 'dreamer', 'enchanted' – marks change in tone from negative to positive.

9. Putting it into practice

Answers should identify at least two further points. For example:
- The narrator is capable of keeping calm and methodical under pressure, as he 'grabbed' the bolt and 'filled my lungs with air'.
- He has a fighting spirit, as he is 'determined to hang on', and also has the self-control to wait for the best moment to let go.

10. Putting it into practice

Answers should identify at least three further points. For example:
- Verbs such as 'handcuffed', 'marched', 'cast' and 'locked up' reflect the prisoner's loss of liberty and lack of choice.
- Nouns with negative connotations, such as 'disease', 'disorder', 'filth' and 'contagion' highlight the conditions the prisoner faces while locked up.
- The repetition of 'he may' emphasises the list of possible horrors that await the prisoner while in prison.

11. The writer's viewpoint

Answers could include the following.
- The writer believes fewer women are voting than men and that this is a problem.
- The writer believes it is important to vote and disagrees with those who, like Russell Brand, encourage people not to vote.
- The reference to the 'UK as a whole' underlines this is a nationwide issue.
- The mention of the 'fast-approaching' election suggests that change is needed now.
- Language such as 'problem', 'greatly' and 'fast approaching' create a sense of urgency.

12. Fact, opinion and expert evidence

Fact: 'One in every two criminals leaving prison will commit another crime within one year of walking out of the prison gates.'
Opinion: 'If the aim of prison is to stop people committing crimes, it's not really working.'
Expert evidence: 'A government analysis puts the improvement at a more conservative 14%.'

13. Explicit information and ideas

Answers should list four things from the text. For example:
- a black dog suffered
- mules flicked flies
- men's stiff collars wilted
- ladies bathed before noon, after their three-o'clock naps.

14. Implicit information and ideas

Answers should identify two pieces of explicit information and two implicit ideas, and could include the following.

Explicit information:
- suffragettes spent their lives campaigning
- suffragettes sacrificed their lives

Implicit ideas:
- it's easy to vote for change ('all we have to do is…')
- the writer thinks it is bad that many people aren't interested in voting ('fight… against voter apathy')

15. Inference

Answers should include and explain two or three short quotations. For example:

- 'gaped' suggests Manderley is wide open and looks vacant or deserted
- 'barrier' suggests the narrator is being prevented from entering
- 'long, tenacious fingers' and 'triumphed' show that nature keeps reaching out and is taking control.

16. Point-Evidence-Explain

For example:
Point: The writer clearly feels frustrated and angry that women do not have the same rights as men.
Evidence: This is revealed when she describes the treatment of women as 'a downright mockery'.
Explanation: The impact of this emotive phrase adds power to her overall argument as it suggests that the law makers are hypocritical for promising liberty while denying women the right to vote. The writer's feelings of injustice are emphasised further through the choice of the negative and colloquial adjective 'downright' and the noun 'mockery'.
You can include more than one piece of evidence to back up a more fully developed point. Stronger answers might also vary the order in which the point, the evidence and the explanation appear, but all these elements should still be present.

17. Putting it into practice

Answers should identify and explain three further points. For example:

- The bows are 'submerged' under 'a great volume of water', making it clear that the ship is sinking.
- The narrator is at the mercy of the power of the water, in danger of being 'swilled back and forth'.
- The choice of the word 'maelstrom' has connotations of dangerous, swirling water that might suck the narrator under.

18. Putting it into practice

Answers should identify and explain three further points. For example:

- The narrator comes home 'shaken in health' but not defeated, encouraging us to admire her strength of character.
- The honesty in the phrase 'bring these egotistical remarks to a close' presents the writer as self-aware and therefore likeable.
- In spite of what she has experienced and the state she has returned home in, she can still take pleasure in 'old familiar faces' and focus on the positive.

19. Word classes

Answers should consist of two sentences and include comments on the use of, for example:

- action verbs to suggest Calpurnia is in control (e.g. 'ordering', 'asking', 'calling')
- the noun 'battle' to show that Scout and Calpurnia's relationship is not an easy one
- adjectives to highlight Calpurnia's strength (e.g. 'hard', 'one-sided').

20. Connotations

Answers could include the following.

- In the phrase 'silent howl', 'silent' literally means there is no sound, while 'howl' suggests an animal-like cry. Here, the phrase suggests that the narrator is feeling a powerful sense of loss and grief but that he is too exhausted or too emotional to let it out fully. It also underlines his powerlessness as he struggles to survive.
- 'chilled' literally means cold. Here, it has connotations of the dangerously icy water the narrator is in and the fear he feels at the sounds of others dying.
- 'ghostly' literally means like a ghost. Here, the connotation is that soon all those in the water will be dead, having no hope of survival, and will become ghosts.

21. Figurative language

Answers should explain how figurative language is used to create atmosphere in the extract. For example:
The writer creates an atmosphere that is both uncomfortable and threatening. The personification of the rhododendrons, which have 'entered into alien marriage', suggests they are in control and have chosen to create this jungle environment. The metaphor 'alien marriage' suggests the union is an unnatural and disturbing one, while the metaphor 'bastard things' reinforces the sense of discomfort and abandonment.

22. Creation of character

Answers could include the following.

- Action – action verbs give a sense of Treelore as industrious ('working', 'lugging') and are also used to describe the unfortunate manner of his death ('slip off', 'fell down', 'crushed').
- Description – Treelore is described as laid back ('slow bout things like that'), academic ('the thinking kind', 'reading all the time'), ambitious ('writing his own book') and hard-working ('working late', 'lugging', 'needed the job', 'tired').

23. Creating atmosphere

1 Answers could include:

- 'gone native now' – the personification of the shrubs suggests danger and gives the impression of an impenetrable jungle
- 'rearing' – a verb with connotations of animal strength
- 'monster height' – an adjective suggesting danger or threat
- 'parasites' – a noun carrying negative connotations of infection and disease.

2 Answers should also include an overview of the overall mood or tone, for example: The overall tone is a menacing one, where nature is threatening and dangerous.

24. Narrative voice

For example:
The writer's choice of first person narration gives the reader a sense of closeness to the narrator. For example, the narrator describes the loss of her son as 'the day my whole world went black' and with the repetition of 'black', 'world' and 'still'. This encourages the reader to sympathise with the narrator and to feel her physical and emotional shock as she 'laid up in bed and stared', which reflects her feelings of paralysis.

25. Putting it into practice

Answers should identify and explain three further points. For example:

- The connotations of 'church' are of somewhere sacred, quiet and still, which adds to the tension of the passage.
- The verbs 'crowded' and 'leant' describe nature as threatening and suggest danger.
- The metaphor 'strange embrace' describing the tangle of branches suggests something uncomfortable and out of place.

26. Putting it into practice

Answers should identify and explain two further points. For example:

- The nouns 'aristocracy' and 'oligarchy' are used as alternatives for 'government' to emphasise the writer's point that the government is not representative of the people and that women are not considered as equals, although they should be.
- The negative nouns in 'dissension, discord, and rebellion', with their connotations of chaos and uprising, are used to show the effects of the inequality between men and women, and act as a warning.

Answers should also include an overview of the overall mood or tone, for example:
The overall tone is a determined one, as the writer puts across her case clearly and logically.

27. Rhetorical devices 1

Answers should identify and explain at least one rhetorical device. For example:
Rhetorical question – 'Are women persons?'. This challenges the audience to disagree and, as they cannot, helps to persuade them that as 'persons', women should be equal to men and be given the right to vote.

28. Rhetorical devices 2

Answers should identify and explain two rhetorical devices. For example:

- Repetition – 'government', 'aristocracy', 'oligarchy'. The writer uses the repetition here to reinforce her point that the government does not represent all people, and that women do not consider it to be a 'democracy' or a 'republic'.
- Contrast – 'rich', 'educated', 'Saxon', 'men sovereigns' are contrasted with 'poor', 'ignorant', 'African', 'women subjects'. These contrasts emphasise how unequal society is and are used to persuade the audience that this is unfair.

29. Whole text structure: fiction

For example:

- Both paragraphs refer to the narrator dreaming.
- In the opening paragraph, the narrator's way is 'barred' but in the ending paragraph the narrator can pass through the barriers.

30. Whole text structure: non-fiction

For example:
The writer engages the reader in the opening section of the text with a detailed description of a typical prisoner's treatment. By listing the horrors that the prisoner is likely to face in the opening paragraph, the writer encourages the reader to sympathise with the prisoner and question whether the treatment can be justified.

31. Identifying sentence types

1 Multi-clause (subordinate)
2 Multi-clause (coordinate)
3 Single-clause
4 Minor

32. Commenting on sentences

For example:
The longer, often multi-clause sentences in the first section of the extract allow the writer to build up a picture of the narrator's son. Similarly, multi-clause sentences are used to bring the focus of the description to the night of his death, helping the reader to visualise the scene. The short, single-clause sentences 'He was tired. It was raining.' provide a contrast and indicate a change of tone before the accident.

33. Putting it into practice

Answers should identify and explain two further points. For example:

- The move from a focus on the narrator's work with children to her own child, who has died, encourages the reader to sympathise with the narrator and to feel a closeness to her.
- The end of the extract shows the narrator as she gets back to work after the death of her son but the reader is left wondering what will happen as we are told a 'bitter seed was planted', which may foreshadow future events.

34. Putting it into practice

For example:
The first paragraph focuses on the treatment of a typical prisoner. The reader is presented with lists of details in emotive language, helping to create a negative picture of the prison system and the effects on the prisoners. In the second paragraph, the focus moves to the effects on wider society, where the writer argues that it is in the law makers' 'own interest' to reform the system.

35. Evaluating a fiction text 1

Annotations should pick up points that examine both sides of the statement. They could include:

- 'she don't pick up her own baby' – suggests Miss Leefolt is uncaring towards her own child
- 'frowning all the time', 'she'd narrow up her eyes at me' – creates impression of someone who is always critical
- 'baby blues', 'worried, like her mama', 'it bother Miss Leefolt' – hints that perhaps Miss Leefolt is struggling or unhappy, rather than simply unpleasant
- Adjectives emphasise a sense of absence, that Miss Leefolt is barely there – 'skinny', 'spindly', 'lanky', 'thin'.
- Adjectives suggest a harsh appearance (and character) – 'pointy chin', 'sharp knobs and corners' – contrasted with 'Babies like fat'.
- 'red devil' – comparison with the devil, use of colour to suggest danger
- 'She try to tease it up, but it only make it look thinner' – mocking tone here makes us feel some sympathy for Miss Leefolt and reflect that the narrator is perhaps being unkind.

36. Evaluating a fiction text 2

For example:
Although Lee introduces Dill as a little pushy and boastful, she also encourages us to have sympathy for him. From the outset, he is eager to show off his reading skills, with 'You got anything needs readin' I can do it'. This suggests he thinks he can do something Jem and Scout can't, which makes him seem a little superior in his attitude and which may lead the reader to view him as arrogant. However, he is also presented as a little defensive in 'I'm little but I'm old', which hints that some of his boastful attitude may actually be hiding nerves, which could result in some readers viewing Dill as insecure. He is also clearly keen to make friends. He is the first to speak and to move closer, 'struggling under the fence', showing that he is brave and perhaps rather desperate to be noticed, which may encourage the reader to sympathise with him.

37. Using evidence to evaluate

For example:
The writer presents the narrator as clearly more experienced with children than Miss Leefolt. The narrator informs the reader that 'I done raised seventeen kids in my lifetime' and lists her skills in all areas of childcare. This is contrasted with the 'terrified' reaction of Miss Leefolt to her own child as she asks the narrator, 'What am I doing wrong? Why can't I stop it?' This, together with the fact that Miss Leefolt is unable to persuade her baby to eat, suggest that she lacks the narrator's experience. The writing is also in the first person, from the personal perspective of the narrator, therefore she is more likely to present herself in a positive light.

38. Putting it into practice

Answers should include one evaluative point. For example:
The number of references to some form of after life, such as 'paradise', 'soul in torment', 'hell' and 'ghostly place' combine to create a strong sense that the narrator is in danger of losing his struggle for survival. This encourages the reader to sympathise with his situation, and admire the courage he displays in fighting on, despite being surrounded by the 'cries', 'lamentations' and 'din of the dying'.

39. Writing about two texts

For example, both texts:

- are about women's right to vote
- refer to the dominant role of men in society
- believe that voting can make a difference.

40. Selecting evidence for synthesis

For example:

- Mary Seacole has returned to England – she is 'wounded' and 'beggared' but alive.

- Captain Scott's future is uncertain: he is still in the Antarctic and experiencing serious problems – frostbite, 'barely a day's fuel' and severe weather.

41. Answering a synthesis question

For example:
Mary Seacole has returned to England following her experience in the Crimean War and while she has returned home 'wounded' and 'beggared', she is alive. On the other hand, Captain Scott's future is uncertain: he is writing from the Antarctic and he and his team are experiencing serious problems including frostbite, 'barely a day's fuel' and severe weather.

42. Looking closely at language

Answers should identify and explain two further points. For example:

- Pattern of three, 'you've lost your job, your flat and possibly your relationship' – used to emphasise the effects of time in prison on prisoners.
- Facts and statistics, '47% of offenders leaving prison reoffend within one year' – used throughout to support the writer's point of view that the prison system doesn't work.

43. Planning to compare language

For example:
Both writers use language to question whether prison has any real impact on the prisoners. Buxton achieves this through hyperbole and emotive language such as 'half-starved', and through the destructive verbs used such as 'exposed' and 'hammered' that graphically highlight the prisoners' harsh treatment. Leach also uses emotive language such as 'lost' and 'don't have any support' to show the effects on the prisoners, though the reader would not be as moved by his account as it is less personal and direct. However, Leach also uses the pattern of three in 'your job, your flat and possibly your relationship' to reinforce his point that prison can have a damaging long-term impact.

44. Comparing language

1 For example: direct address, varied sentence length for effect
2 and 3 For example:

- Both sources use lists of negative effects to make the point that the prison system needs improvement. Buxton focuses more heavily on the effects on the typical prisoner as he is 'handcuffed… marched… followed… and exposed', which encourages the reader to sympathise with the prisoner and agree with Buxton. On the other hand, Leach uses lists to point out the problems with the system, where restorative justice is not an option for 'domestic violence, murder or rape'.
- **Similarly**, both texts use repetition for emphasis. While Buxton uses the repetition of 'He may', for example, to reinforce the horrors of prison life, Leach uses subheadings to repeat and highlight key facts and statistics in his article, such as 'Community sentences reduce reoffending by 6%'. In both texts, this use of language helps to persuade the reader to agree with the writer.

45. Comparing structure

For example:
Source 5a, *The state of the Prisons, 1818*: The opening engages the reader's sympathy by focusing on the treatment of a typical prisoner and painting a negative picture of prison life; the final paragraph moves to a focus on how the prison system has negative consequences for society, which helps to persuade the reader that the system needs to change.
Source 5b, 'Prison doesn't work': The opening paragraph presents the writer's viewpoint that the prison system doesn't work, supported by facts and statistics. The article ends on a similar note, using statistics to persuade the reader that the system needs to be improved.

46. Comparing ideas

For example:

- Similarity in language: Both writers use a rhetorical question in their final paragraph, to make sure the reader focuses on the key point that women should vote.
- Difference in language: Susan Anthony uses repetition of key words such as 'oligarchy' to underline her view that the current system is unfair; Flo Henry supports her opinions with statistics such as 'only 64% of women' to reinforce her argument that not enough women are using their right to vote.
- Similarity in structure: Both writers begin by encouraging the reader to support their viewpoints, engaging the reader from the opening paragraph.
- Difference in structure: Susan Anthony starts with specific reference to her own voting experience, which sets the context for her speech, and ends by talking about women's right to vote generally, to emphasise this is a wider issue; Flo Henry begins by engaging the reader in the historical context of women's right to vote and ends with a call to action, encouraging her readers to register to vote.

47. Comparing perspective

For example:
Susan Anthony opens her speech with the view that by voting she has simply 'exercised my citizen's rights'. This is also her view in the final paragraph, where she argues that women are 'persons' and therefore 'citizens', so should have the right to vote. Similarly, Flo Henry begins her article with the idea that it is important for women to vote 'to change some of the policies that constrain us'; she maintains this viewpoint throughout, encouraging her readers to vote in her closing paragraph, 'to restore some of the suffragette enthusiasm'.

48. Answering a comparison question

For example:
Both texts are about how the prison system is ineffective, but Buxton aims to highlight the conditions in the prison and the effects on both prisoners and society, while Leach emphasises the failure of the prison system to reduce reoffending. Both writers use lists for emphasis. Buxton paints a vivid picture to persuade the reader to agree with him by listing in detail what the typical prisoner will experience when he is convicted; for example, how he will be forced to mix with the worst of society and 'adopt their habits, their language and their sentiments'. Similarly, Leach uses lists for effect, as in 'domestic violence, murder or rape', although here the tone is less emotive and the list is used to deliver key facts about restorative justice rather than try to encourage an emotional response in the way Buxton does.

49. Putting it into practice

Answers could include the following.

- Both writers contrast men and women: Susan Anthony ('all men sovereigns, all women subjects') to point out the inequality and to reinforce her argument that women should be treated as equals and be allowed to vote; Flo Henry to suggest that more women should be using their right to vote.
- Both writers suggest that the inequality in voting rights is a problem for everyone: Susan Anthony through her repetition of 'we'; Flo Henry in 'politicians and citizens alike'.
- Both writers keep their perspective throughout, though Susan Anthony moves from the personal to the wider issue of votes for women, while Flo Henry opens with the historical context to emphasise the importance of not wasting the vote.
- Both writers use a rhetorical question in their final paragraph: Susan Anthony to conclude her argument that women are equals and deserve the vote; Flo Henry to rally her readers to vote in the next election.
- Susan Anthony uses repetition of key words such as 'oligarchy' to underline her view that the current system is

unfair; Flo Henry supports her opinions with statistics such as 'only 64% of women' to reinforce her argument that not enough women are using their right to vote.

- Susan Anthony makes the case that women should have an equal right to vote by listing inequalities ('the rich govern the poor') while Flo Henry thinks 'we need to fight for feminism' and that women cannot only be equal because there are issues that 'purely affect women'.

SECTION B: WRITING

50. Writing questions: an overview

1 Paper 2
2 One writing question
3 Both papers

51. Writing questions: Paper 1

Purpose – creative writing competition, so write creatively to engage and entertain the reader
Audience – students from own year group
Form – narrative, but only the opening of the story
Answers should also include at least 5 or 6 ideas, for example:

- being evacuated to countryside from city
- woken up early, everything a hurry
- on a train station in crowd, uses senses to describe the scene
- feel scared, don't want to be separated from parents
- with sister, holding her hand tightly
- boarding train, losing sight of mother.

52. Writing question: Paper 2

Purpose – argue for or against statement given in order to present own viewpoint
Audience – headteacher
Form – letter
Answers should also include at least 5 or 6 ideas, for example:

- mobile phones can be disruptive, but can also be used to learn
- students less focused as distracted, quality of work suffers
- noise a problem, interrupts learning
- risk of theft or damage to phones, cause of tension
- potential for bullying if use of phones encouraged
- can be used to access online resources to support learning, e.g. dictionaries.

53. Writing questions: time management

Responses will vary, but should be in the form of a 140-character tweet and include the key points such as:

- check time available for the question
- stay focused on the question
- pause, breathe and review work regularly
- plan before writing, proofread work at end.

54. Writing for a purpose: creative 1

For example: The dark closed around me as the door clicked shut. I rattled the handle and, as I realised it was locked, a shudder climbed up my spine.
(**Note** the use of the senses (*dark, clicked, rattled*); the physical symptoms of fear (*shudder*); and the use of personification (*climbed*)).

55. Writing for a purpose: creative 2

For example:
His quivering nostrils widened momentarily. The thick, fragrant air hit the back of his throat and threw him off balance. Reaching out, Matthew closed his hand around the ledge of smooth, polished wood in front of him, his knuckles as rigid as the pew itself. As he kept his eyes on the unforgiving stone beneath his feet, swaying as each new wave of terror rolled through his stomach, he listened to the low murmur around him. A simmering air of expectation.
(**Note** the use of the senses (*thick, fragrant, smooth, murmur*); the physical symptoms of fear (*quivering, rigid, swaying*); the use of personification (*hit, threw*); the use of simile (*as rigid as*); the use of verbs and adverbs (*momentarily, rolled*); unusual adjectives (*unforgiving, simmering*).)

56. Writing for a purpose: viewpoint 1

1 For example: Many of those who enter these shows do not display any real gift or talent; many entrants have surprisingly low self-esteem, which is then further destroyed by the experience; talent shows are more about laughing at others than about celebrating real ability.
2 For example: It is true that some have found fame as a result of entering a talent show, but the fame is often short-lived and winners are often taken advantage of by unscrupulous corporations only interested in making money.
3 For example:
For a lucky few, fame, fortune and a fantastic future beckon. (alliteration/pattern of three)
Can a competition that mocks its competitors be a positive experience for anyone? (rhetorical question)
One minute the winner is riding high on the wave of success, the next they are sinking under the glare of negative publicity. (hyperbole, contrast)

57. Writing for a purpose: viewpoint 2

1 For example: I would use an informal register to suggest a friendly voice, but with standard English to suggest the information is reliable and trustworthy.
2 For example: Research suggests the majority of teenagers feel under pressure to look, feel or act in a particular way; more than 50% of teenagers have experienced some form of bullying; teenagers are less likely to behave aggressively if they feel they have their parents' support.
3 For example: Do you know how your teenager is feeling? According to a recent survey, more than 75% of parents are out of touch with their children's lives and find it difficult to offer the support and understanding their children need.

58. Writing for an audience

For example: You may think you've got ages to prepare for your GCSEs. You may think you don't need to worry about them just yet. But time flies and it won't be long before you're sitting in that exam hall. So it's important to start getting ready for them now.
(**Note** the use of some informal features, e.g. abbreviations such as 'you've', which are appropriate to this audience but would not be in a more formal text.)

59. Putting it into practice

For example:
Timing plan: 45 mins total: 5 mins planning; 35 mins writing; 5 mins checking
Purpose: creative writing for English department wall display, so write imaginatively to engage and entertain the reader
Audience: the English department staff, other students in the school, teachers, possibly parents and other visitors
Form: description
Narrative voice: first person
Initial ideas: describe standing next to girl at bus stop; girl leaves coat on seat with wallet inside; miss own bus to take wallet to address; house with eerie, ghostlike atmosphere, shivers down spine; find out girl died three years before.

60. Putting it into practice

For example:
Purpose: to present my point of view, so I will mainly need to argue and persuade
Audience: readers of a broadsheet newspaper, so mainly adults
Form: article
Own point of view: beaches a disgrace, important to work together to clean them up and prevent future littering and pollution

61. Form: articles

Responses will vary, but should:

- sum up key ideas in paragraph 1
- give more detail in paragraph 2
- include a quotation in paragraph 3

62. Form: letters and reports

1 Letter (formal)
2 Report
3 Letter (informal)

63. Form: speeches

Responses will vary, but should consist of two paragraphs and include some of these speech writing techniques:

- Rhetorical devices
- Facts and opinions
- Counter-arguments
- Key points clearly signposted with adverbials
- Personal examples
- Short, direct statements
- Challenges addressed and solutions offered

64. Putting it into practice

For example:
Headline – Teenagers of Today: Rebels or Role Models
Subheading – A local teenager reveals the truth about our young people
Short opening paragraph – It has recently been claimed that the teenagers in our community are agents of trouble, intent on bad behaviour and making a nuisance of themselves. It is a picture many of us are willing to believe, yet does it paint the whole truth?
Developed paragraph – There are of course those who think it does. However, at the end of my road, in a small, unassuming house, lives a young person who defies this image of dangerous delinquent on a daily basis. Jemima Johnson acts not for recognition or for praise, or because she was asked to help. Jemima acts because she has noticed someone in need and has understood that she can make a difference. What does she do? Every day, Jemima accompanies her elderly neighbour to the local shop, providing Mrs Forbes with an arm to lean on, the chance for a little daily exercise and a hand with the groceries. Of Jemima, Mrs Forbes says, "She is an angel. I don't know what I'd do without her". And Jemima is not alone.

65. Ideas and planning: creative

Plans should include four or five key ideas and a range of supporting details, including appropriate creative writing techniques.

66. Structure: creative

Plans should use the narrative structure and include supporting details about creative writing techniques.

67. Beginnings and endings: creative

For example:

1 Opening 1 (vivid description) – The house sat still and silent, squatting low as if to keep out winter's stinging embrace as the dark night pressed forward, its penetrating stare painting the windows black as coal. Inside…
Opening 2 (dialogue) – "What was that?" squeaked Adam, his eyes wide with fright, his brow furrowed.
"I don't know," breathed Henry, the quivering syllables leaving his lips in a whisper…
Opening 3 (mystery) – I know now that it was a mistake. A big one. I should have left things as they were – peaceful, familiar, safe. And yet, that evening…
Opening 4 (conflict or danger) – A whining creak. A floorboard. Where were they? I could see nothing in the pitch and edged around the doorframe into the hall…

2 Ending (to Opening 1) – I was glad, then, and after all that had passed, to be cradled as I was in the peaceful dark. The night was now familiar to me, its hold as comforting as the arms of an old friend. As I stretched out my tired limbs and pulled the blanket closer to me, I closed my eyes, my lips falling into a sleepy smile. It was good to be home.

68. Putting it into practice

For example:
Resolution – [describe examining the package and then finding, on the back 'until the morning']; suspect it's from friend, a surprise for tomorrow's trip out; use five senses to describe package; open package; it's a silly hat, with a note, from friend to wear to fair as planned; stranger was friend's uncle, who offered to drop off the package; metaphor to describe hat.
First two paragraphs of the answer should follow the plan on page 68 and use one or more of the techniques from page 67.

69. Ideas and planning: viewpoint 1

A possible plan:

- Introduction – hundreds of channels, 24 hours a day, television can dominate.
- Point 1 – TV can be informative/educational.
- Point 2 – shared experience of high quality drama, etc. (no different to theatre but cheaper and more accessible).
- Counter-argument: some say it takes over our lives; they need to learn how to turn it off.
- Conclusion: like anything, TV is good and bad; it depends on how it's used. Used carefully/selectively it can bring people together, entertain, inform and educate.

70. Ideas and planning: viewpoint 2

For example:
Intro:

- Give overview of situation – young people have more exams to take than ever before, and schools are under pressure to continue raising grades; this creates extreme stress; schools not doing enough to help
- Key point – How teenagers feel and how they act
- Anxious and nervous about the exams
- Confused about how to approach revision
- Tired due to sleepless nights caused by worrying
- Key point – What the school can do
- Set up special study zones
- Provide study sessions outside normal school hours
- Help students create a revision timetable
- Offer relaxation sessions to help calm and focus the mind
- Key point – Support needed
- School year group team
- Revision materials and guidance on the school website
- Older students
- Conclusion – Finally…
- Plan some kind of celebration for results day
- Ensure all students are recognised for their achievements
- Reminder about benefits to school if students do well

71. Openings: viewpoint

1 For example:

- Do we ever question the purpose of school? Or do we just go there every day because we have to?
- Exam results can affect our future, but the experience of school can change our lives forever.
- Nearly half of 16-year-olds in the UK do not achieve five good passes at GCSE.

2 **Exam results can affect our future, but the experience of school can change our lives forever.** While Year 11 students are constantly subjected to their teachers panicking about looming exams, we should remember how relatively unimportant those exams really are. School does not just teach us enough maths and geography to get a GCSE or two. School helps teach us how to live in the world.
(**Note** that the bold opening sentence is developed and justified in the remainder of the paragraph as the writer's argument is introduced and outlined: exams are unimportant; school teaches us much more than how to pass them.)

72 Conclusions: viewpoint

For example: It is important to work hard at school, to achieve the best results we can for our own satisfaction – but the lessons we learn about being with other people, about setting goals and working towards them, about cooperation and survival will stay with us forever. School days may not be the happiest days of our lives; but they can teach us how to be healthy and happy with ourselves and each other for the rest of our lives. And isn't that more important than a handful of A*s?

(**Note** the first sentence of this conclusion summarises the writer's argument; the second adds a positive note; the final sentence asks a rhetorical question, further promoting their argument.)

73. Putting it into practice

Effective plans will include:

- ideas for an introduction and conclusion
- a range of key points
- some developed detail for each key point
- key points logically sequenced.

Opening paragraphs will vary but should reflect the content of the plan.

74. Paragraphing

If students choose to add a paragraph to the first example they should use Point-Evidence-Explain.

If they have added a paragraph to the second example they need to have clearly introduced the reader to the content of the paragraph then developed it and added detail.

75. Linking ideas

For example:

This morning, my sister proved that she is the most annoying person on earth. **Firstly**, she finished all the milk so there was none left for me. **Then** she spent an hour in the bathroom. **Finally**, she borrowed my headphones without asking and wouldn't give them back. **On the other hand**, she can be thoughtful. **For example**, she made me a delicious lasagne the other day. **Similarly**, she always remembers my birthday and buys me great presents.

76. Putting it into practice

Effective answers will:

- be structured using Point-Evidence-Explain
- sequence and signal their ideas using a range of adverbials.

77. Formality and standard English 1

For example:

You may think that making a living is easy. You may believe that you don't need to make any effort at all in order to earn a respectable salary. This is an illusion. The key to a successful career is hard work. Make sure you revise thoroughly and start early. Effective revision takes time.

78. Formality and standard English 2

For example:

Replace slang – e.g change 'gut' to 'instinct'

Replace colloquial language – e.g. change 'Is there any chance' to 'Would you consider', 'Would you be prepared to' or 'Is there a possibility of'

Replace informal, texting language – e.g. change 'gr8' to 'an impressive contribution to the local community'

Replace unsophisticated vocab – e.g. change 'give' to 'offer', 'good' to 'keen', 'sure' to 'confident'

Replace adjective 'enthusiastic attitude' with 'enthusiasm'

Replace active voice – e.g. change 'My English teacher says' to 'I am told', 'I will impress you' to 'you will be impressed'

79 Vocabulary for effect: synonyms

For example: The idea of celebrities as perfect role models is not the only misguided ~~idea~~ concept connected with the world of the ~~celebrity~~ famous. Some people have the ~~idea~~ notion that ~~celebrities~~ superstars should be consulted on everything from international politics to haircare.

80. Vocabulary for effect: creative

For example: A bead of sweat trickled down my forehead and ran into my eye. My eyelid flickered, twitching anxiously as it blinked away the pain. I could feel my shirt stuck to the sweat pooling on my back and the tremor in my stomach becoming a violent jolting. It was getting closer.

(**Note** how this response focuses closely on the physical symptoms of the feeling of fear, but does not yet reveal the cause of it, hoping to intrigue the reader.)

81. Vocabulary for effect: viewpoint

For example: In the UK at this very moment hundreds of children, some as young as five, are being kept in appalling conditions. They are caged for up to seven hours a day. They are often made to sit in silence while aggressive adults hurl abuse at them. They are subjected to a ruthless regime of punishments. Most shockingly of all, this brutal and barbaric treatment is accepted as normal despite the suffering it causes.

Note:

- the use of negative emotive language (*appalling, ruthless,* etc.) to emphasise the paragraph's central idea
- language chosen for its connotations of imprisonment and torture (*caged, brutal, barbaric*).

82. Language for different effects 1

Paper 1, for example:

- Rhetorical question – Could there be anywhere more perfect or serene?
- Contrast – In the harbour, just off the coast of the noisy, bustling centre of Poole lies the peaceful haven that is Brownsea Island.
- List – I walked along the deserted beach, collecting shells, skimming stones and breathing in the salty sea air.
- Repetition – The island was quiet. The island was peaceful. The island was gloriously deserted.

Paper 2, for example:

- Rhetorical question – Do you want to live a long and healthy life?
- Contrast – Roaming the great outdoors and breathing lungfuls of fresh air in the sunshine is much more enjoyable than sitting in a stale, airless room staring mindlessly at the television.
- List – Obesity can increase your risk of diabetes, heart attack, depression, arthritis, liver failure, and breathing difficulties.
- Repetition – Exercise can improve your health. Exercise can improve your happiness. Exercise can change your life.

83. Language for different effects 2

Paper 1, for example:

- Direct address – You would never believe the pressure my mum inflicted on me.
- Pattern of three – She nagged, pestered and hounded me for days.
- Hyperbole – I thought my head was going to explode.
- Alliteration – This was going to be the most miserable minute of my entire life.

Paper 2, for example:

- Direct address – I would ask you to consider the substantial benefits of under-16s being allowed to own a mobile phone.
- Pattern of three – Owning a mobile phone can help under-16s to build a healthy social life, learn to manage the costs involved and stay safe.
- Hyperbole – Preventing under-16s from owning a mobile phone would not only be unfair; it would also snatch from them any chance of a normal life and condemn them to life as social outcasts.
- Alliteration – For parents serious about safety, mobile phones are essential equipment for the under-16s.

84. Language for different effects 3

Paper 1, for example:
Simile – I stared up at her in awe: she was **like a Greek goddess**.
Metaphor – She **was an oasis of calm** amidst the chaos and clamour.
Personification – Her **kind words touched** my heart.

Paper 2, for example:
Simile – For many young people, childhood is **like a race** which should be won as soon as possible.
Metaphor – Childhood **is a rare and precious jewel** which we should treasure.
Personification – This relentless pressure **batters children** and their childhood into the ground.

85. Putting it into practice

Effective answers should include:

- a range of well-chosen and varied vocabulary
- simile, metaphor and personification used **appropriately** and **sparingly**
- a range of language techniques for effect.

86. Putting it into practice

Effective answers should include:

- a counter-argument
- adverbials to link key points and paragraphs
- a wide and varied vocabulary
- simile, metaphor and personification, if used **sparingly**
- some use of appropriate techniques, such as alliteration, facts, opinions.

87. Sentence variety 1

Single-clause sentence – My new bedroom is tiny.
Multi-clause sentence with a subordinate clause – Although I was looking forward to the move, I knew I would miss my friends terribly.
Multi-clause sentence with a coordinate clause – My brother got to ride in the removal van but I went in the car with the others.
Multi-clause sentence with a relative clause – Our new house, which is much bigger than the cramped house I grew up in, is in a quiet cul-de-sac.
Minor sentence – Lovely.

88. Sentence variety 2

For example:
Pronoun – I was waiting alone in a classroom.
Article – An eerie silence had fallen.
Preposition – Beyond the classroom door, I heard footsteps.
-ing word – Holding my breath, I waited.
Adjective – Empty and cold, the classroom did nothing to comfort me.
Adverb – Slowly I realised there was a man standing in the doorway.
Conjunction – Although I had never seen him before, I knew immediately why he was there.

89. Sentences for different effects

For example:

- Life, many people say, is a game for winners and, if you are not a winner, you are a loser who has not worked hard enough or focused clearly enough on your goals. They could not be more wrong.

(**Note** that the first sentence has been intentionally extended using multiple clauses.)

- Whether I'm playing Monopoly, taking a test or running the hundred metres, I always come last.

(**Note** how the key information is placed in the final clause.)

90. Putting it into practice

Effective answers should:

- use a range of single-clause, multi-clause and minor sentences
- use a range of sentence lengths
- start sentences in a variety of ways
- feature sentences structured for effect.

91. Ending a sentence

The corrections are shown in bold. For example:
I was born in the countryside **and** I grew up surrounded by the sounds and smells of the natural world**.** **W**hen I was ten we moved to the city**.** **It** was a confusing, fast-paced, deafening environment that I found hard to love. It was such a big change **– and** it came as quite a shock to my system**.** **W**orst of all I had to leave all my friends behind and try to make new ones in this strange, unfamiliar place. I was lonely **and** convinced I would never feel at home **but** before a year had passed I had the best friend anyone could wish for.

92. Commas

For example:

- List – Nursery school**,** primary school**,** middle school and secondary school make up a large proportion of our early lives.
- Main + subordinate clause – Although there may be difficult moments**,** the friendships we make at school can last a lifetime.
- Main + relative clause – Those difficult moments**,** which seem terrible at the time**,** are easily outnumbered by the happy ones.

93. Apostrophes and speech punctuation

The corrections are shown in bold.
'There**'**s nothing I can do**,'** said Gary**'**s dad.
'Are you sure**?'** **r**eplied Gary.
'I don**'**t know what you mean**,'** **s**aid his dad.
'I think you do**.'**

94. Colons, semi-colons, dashes, brackets and ellipses

1 A colon.
2 A semi-colon.
3 To add, mid-sentence, information that is extra but not entirely necessary.

95. Putting it into practice

Effective answers should include a range of accurate punctuation including commas, apostrophes, colons and semi-colons.

96. Common spelling errors 1

Are students spotting all their spelling mistakes?

97. Common spelling errors 2

The corrections are shown in bold.
I saw Annabel walk **past** wearing **your** shoes. She was carrying **your** bag **too**. I don't know **whose** coat she had on but it had **two** stripes across the back. She stopped and took it **off**. I don't know **where** she was going or what she was up **to**. It was very strange.

98. Common spelling errors 3

Are students using effective strategies to learn words?

99. Proofreading

Are students spotting errors in their writing?

100. Putting it into practice

Effective answers should contain at least five corrected mistakes.